The Novels of Toni Morrison

American University Studies

Series XXIV
American Literature

Vol. 31

PETER LANG
New York • San Francisco • Bern
Frankfurt am Main • Berlin • Wien • Paris

Patrick Bryce Bjork

The Novels of Toni Morrison

The Search for Self and Place
Within the Community

PETER LANG
New York • San Francisco • Bern
Frankfurt am Main • Berlin • Wien • Paris

Library of Congress Cataloging-in-Publication Data

Bjork, Patrick Bryce.
　The novels of Toni Morrison: the search for self and place within
the community / Patrick Bryce Bjork.
　　p.　cm. — (American university studies. Series XXIV, American
literature ; vol. 31)
　　Includes bibliographical references (p.　)
　　1. Morrison, Toni—Criticism and interpretation. 2. Afro-
Americans in literature. 3. Community life in literature. 4. Self in
literature. I. Title. II. Series.
PS3563.08749Z56　　1992, 1994　　813'.54—dc20　　91–34571
ISBN 0-8204-1779-3　　　　　　　　　　　　　　　CIP
ISBN 0-8204-2569-9 (pbk)
ISSN 0895-0512

Die Deutsche Bibliothek-CIP-Einheitsaufnahme

Bjork, Patrick Bryce.
　The novels of Toni Morrison: the search for self and place within
the community / Patrick Bryce Bjork—New York; Berlin; Bern;
Frankfurt/M.; Paris; Wien: Lang, 1992, 1994
　　(American university studies: Ser. 24, American literature; Vol. 31)
　　ISBN 0-8204-1779-3
　　ISBN 0-8204-2569-9 (pbk)
NE: American university studies/24

The paper in this book meets the guidelines for permanence and
durability of the Committee on Production Guidelines for Book
Longevity of the Council on Library Resources.

Second Printing

Contents

Preface

The search for self and place is an on-going phenomenon in American discourse. Our current speech and writing are suffused with expressions and images of "finding one's self" and establishing one's "space." Often Americans view this search as an age-old concern so that across the span of human history, both oral and written discourse appear to speak to a desire for a fully realized identity and place. In short, our lives and literature, both past and present, have been frequently defined by the desire to create and uncreate ourselves and our places within and without the human community.

Perhaps nowhere is the American search for self and place more carefully concentrated than in our national literature. For any given author, be it Hawthorne or Chopin, Faulkner or McCullers, the questions, "Who am I?" and "Where do I belong?" often form the basis for a traditional exegesis. And thus, one might not read, for instance, *The Awakening* or *The Heart Is a Lonely Hunter* without in some way acknowledging this search as a determinant in character and plot development. Much critical analysis also centers upon the role self and place play in American literature. R.W.B. Lewis' *The American Adam* or Barbara Christian's "Community and Nature: The Novels of Toni Morrison" are just two of the scores of critical pieces that testify to this on-going concern for self and place.

My analyses of Toni Morrison's novels are grounded in this American phenomenon. Yet Morrison's novels demonstrate a different kind of search than many American readers are accustomed to. Morrison's work consistently shows that identity and place are found in the community and in the communal experience, and not in the transcendence of society or in the search for a single, private self. It is this central difference that attracts me most to Toni Morrison.

Generally speaking, American life and literature are marked by an intrinsic and critical ideology based on our notions of individualism. American discourse, both past and present, public and private, revels in individual spirit and assertion, and many Americans show great respect for those individuals who have been able to "go it alone," to survive the odds, to "pull themselves up by their bootstraps." Paradoxically, this ideology knits much of our society together and forms an inspirational, devotional bond that keeps us striving to "be all that [we] can be." Thus, many Americans have learned to appreciate and accept the romantic appeal of being self-reliant, of transcending society, and ultimately defining a single, private self.

In her essay, "City Limits, Village Values," Morrison writes that

> . . . [white] critics tend not to trust or respect a hero who prefers the village and its tribal values to heroic loneliness and alienation. When a character defies a village law or shows contempt for its values, it may be seen as a triumph to white readers, while Blacks may see it as an outrage. (38)

What Morrison writes of here is almost entirely foreign, even distasteful to many Americans. Finding and accepting identity within the group, the clan, the neighborhood smacks of a conformity that has received endless debunking in white literature and literary criticism. So much so that, as John M. Reilly asserts in his "History-Making Literature," ". . . the bourgeois values of individualism become presuppositions with the appearance of probability certified by repetition in hundreds of stories."

I vividly recall a high school American novel class that in every way underscored these "presuppositions." We read novels by Dreiser and Lewis and Hemingway and Salinger, and the recurring message, both explicit and implied, was that conformity to the group leads to mediocrity and malaise. For the black writer writing during the same period as the above writers, he or she could and often would tap into this ideology of bourgeois individualism in an attempt to form fiction that reflected and accommodated a presumed historical world. As

Reilly states, "the [black] writer [could] be misled into relying on many of these presuppositions, because he or she [could] not find satisfactory plots for Black experience. . . ." But as Reilly goes on to say, "authentically complete fiction . . . requires . . . an outlook or episteme that can appropriate to literature the contradictions of history as it is lived beyond the page" (111).

In Morrison's *Song of Solomon*, the protagonist embarks on a quest for identity—a story which, from childhood onward, I have read in countless variations. But unlike much mainstream, bourgeois American literature, this protagonist learns that identity is not found in the self, alone and apart from the group; instead, he discovers that "you just can't fly off and leave a body." Each communal variation, the community, the clan, the ancestor, is an intrinsic part of the self, and exists not merely as an altruistic concern.

Here is a primary contradiction in American cultural history, for as Houston A. Baker points out in his *Long Black Song*:

> Black American culture is characterized by a collectivistic ethos; society is not viewed as [an] . . . arena in which the individual can work out his own destiny and gain a share of America's benefits by his own efforts. To the black American these benefits are not attained solely by individual efforts, but by changes in the nature of society and the social, economic, and political advancement of a whole race of people. . . . (16)

Therefore, one should not leave unacknowledged the worth of and the need for the group's values, beliefs, and customs. To do so, to transcend and/or to repudiate the community, merely discontinues dialogue and diminishes the potential for cultural regeneration.

The community is paramount in not just Morrison's work but also in many 20th-century novels written by black women. Their narratives reflect a cultural reality within any given black neighborhood. Like any disenfranchised group, there is, to quote Morrison, ". . . joy and protection in the clan" (38) and historically, black women have played an integral role in perpetuating this bonding process. Traditionally their positions in both white and black patriarchy have been relegated to domestic, familial concerns. Thus, a narrative preoccupation with clan and community documents black women's creative sharing of self through story and song in order to demonstrate how dialogue and reciprocity provide the basis for identity and cultural regeneration. As a result, many black women's novels provide an affront to "pre-supposed" American literature through their affirmation of collective experience. Each of Morrison's novels demonstrates what the community can or should offer to its members by way of identity and place. And although a protagonist may reject community, there remains a utopian desire to create an identity with and among others in hopes of alleviating the alienation, loneliness, and stasis learned and felt by the privatized American self.

In order to provide a critical and cultural context for Morrison's work, I have included two introductory chapters. The first chapter details a short history of the African-American novel and discusses the subsequent criticism surrounding it. Chapter Two discusses in more detail the communal and regenerative roles that black women play in the community and how those roles are or have been incorporated into African-American narratives. My overall purpose in both chapters is to trace the emergence and presence of critical and cultural values in black American literature and to show how they have influenced such contemporary black women writers as Toni Morrison.

In the remaining chapters, I discuss each of Morrison's novels by examining how cultural and communal values, beliefs, and customs contribute to a protagonist's search for identity and place. In each novel, Morrison demonstrates that the self is always and forever inextricably linked to the community. Continually, in thought, word, or deed, its members return to the community, the neighborhood, the clan to become shaped and/or misshaped by their reciprocating influence. As a result, in myth and memory, folktale and song, Morrison weaves her complex narratives to underscore her belief that "without that presence and recognition [of community] there is no life" (43).

To Raymond

Chapter I

The Search for Individual Talent and the Continuity of Tradition

Any extended study in black literature should, in the words of Robert B. Stepto, attempt to "mediate between individual talent and the continuity of (literary) tradition" (22). To accomplish this Stepto suggests that one must "illuminate the historical consciousness of an art form" (20) by examining the landscape of literary and authorial history revealed within and around any given text. This particular notion of intertextuality, of how texts respond to other texts, is especially pertinent to black literary studies.

Until very recently, black literary studies remained grounded in social or historical commentary; its locus of concentration rested on content rather than the interplay between content and form. But as Henry Louis Gates, Jr. now maintains, "literary images, even black ones, are combinations of words, not of absolute or fixed things." And thus, as Gates continues, "the tendency of black criticism toward an ideological absolutism, with its attendant Inquisition, must come to an end" (68).

"Mediation" and intertextuality, then, will enable one to sustain a closer reading of black literature, and, for this study, to more fully illuminate the novels of Toni Morrison. But we may wonder why and how current African-American criticism arrived at this denouement.

Beginning with the 19th century slave narratives (1830-1861), the African-American text established itself as a medium of propaganda. These narratives were produced under the guidance and approval of white abolitionists and sold extraordinarily well to a Northern white audience. However, the popularity of these narratives was based more upon Americans' insatiable desire for Cooper-like, Western tales of long and perilous journeys than upon genuine abolitionist sympathies. Thus, from its inception, the African-American text developed unwittingly as a literary institution that generated the values of the dominant culture. As a consequence, the ruling social order began its control of African-American literary production.

During Reconstruction, the African-American text, continued to reproduce the values of the dominant society by creating palatable conventions and stereotypes for a predominantly white audience. For instance, Booker T. Washington's *Up From Slavery* essentially reproduced the myth of the Protestant work ethic. Its overwhelming acceptance by white readers indicated that the ruling ideology was able to appropriate it. At the same time, of course, the same ruling ideology and literary establishment repressed any genuine representations of black culture, such as oral narratives or work songs. Instead, the single most recurring stereotype in black Reconstruction literature became the tragic mulatta.

While white southern literature produced their own black stereotype, the mammy, the Aunt Jemima, the nurturing double to the pedestaled southern white woman, African-American writers, even before the Civil War, developed the tragic mulatta. Two of its most prominent representations were *Clotell* (1853) by William Wells Brown and Francis E. W. Harper's *Iola LeRoy* (1892), the first published novel by a black woman. The purpose of these and other novels was the uplifting of the black race. But it was an uplift which was approved and accommodated by the dominant culture.

The mulatta, a product of a black slave mother and a white slave master, denied the long-time philosophical concept that blacks were subhuman. In *Clotell* and *Iola LeRoy*, the mulatta is depicted as beautiful, courageous, and refined much in the same way as her mistress. Her tragedy is that while she sees the power and pleasures of the master's house, she cannot share in those advantages of the dominant culture.

But what seems especially important is that white readers, according to Barbara Christian in her work, *Black Feminist*

Criticism, accepted and accommodated the mulatta novels by misreading them:

> White audiences lapped up the stories of the mulattas and their tragedies in the ironic way that the guilty and powerful always delight in looking obliquely at their guilt. The existence of the mulatta, who combined the physical characteristics of both races, denied their claim that blacks were not human, while allowing them the argument that they were lifting up the race by lightening it. (3)

But of even greater significance was that the mulatta woman rather than the man was chosen to project this image. This is another example of dominant culture accommodation, for as Christian goes on to say, "Woman in white culture is not as powerful as man, so to pose the existence of a mulatto slave man who embodies the qualities of the master is so great a threat, so dangerous an idea, even in fiction, that it is seldom tried" (4). Not only do we see, then, the dominant culture's ironic accommodation of this racial stereotype, and thus its overt racism, but also a racism coupled with sexism—a double-edged sword which black women, to the present, continue to encounter.

Aiding in the production and repression of the African-American text was white literary criticism. Even before the slave narratives, criticism of the African-American text exerted a prescriptive influence. One glaring example of this early white prescriptiveness was Thomas Jefferson's Notes on the State of Virginia (1787) wherein he discussed the poetry of the black slave woman, Phillis Wheatley. Of her poetry Jefferson writes,

> Never yet could I find a Black that had uttered a thought above the level of plain narrative; never seen even an elementary trait of painting or sculpture. The compositions published under her name are below the dignity of criticism. (196).

Jefferson's polemic reaffirmed the dominant culture's belief that blacks would need to achieve physical unity with whites or forever remain limited both mentally and thus artistically. As Jefferson goes on to assert: ". . . the improvement of the blacks in body and mind, in the first instance of their mixture with the whites, has been observed by every one, and proves that their inferiority is not the effect merely of their condition of life" (196).

While Jefferson's desire for race, and thus white, unity was obviously never realized, the dominant culture, in subsequent years, modified its accommodation and/or repression of black art to what William Dean Howells called "white thinking and white feeling." Howells, in reviewing Paul Laurence Dunbar's *Majors and Minors*, had this to say about black art and humanity:

> If his Minors (the dialect pieces) had been written by a white man I should have been struck by their uncommon quality; I should have said that they were wonderful divinations. But since they are expressions of a race-life from within the race, they seem to me infinitely more valuable and significant. I have sometimes fancied that perhaps the negroes thought black, and felt black: that they were racially so utterly alien and distinct from ourselves that there never could be common intellectual and emotional ground between us, and that whatever eternity might do to reconcile us, the end of time would find us far asunder as ever. But this little book, has given me pause in my speculation. Here in the artistic effect at least, is white thinking and white feeling in a black man, and perhaps the human unity, and not the race unity, is the precious thing, the divine thing, after all. God hath made of one blood all nations of men: perhaps the proof of this saying is to appear in the arts, and our hostilities and prejudices are to vanish in them. (251)

Within Howell's discourse there exists much of what constitutes all subsequent white criticism of African-American literature. By prefacing his observation with a discussion on physical and spiritual blackness, Howells presupposes that blackness may be a "valuable and significant" criterion for criticism. But since it is "so utterly alien" to the white dominant position, it must also be, by inference, a disenfranchised or secondary position. Therefore, in order for the African-American text to achieve a primary position, Howells recommends a one-sided adaptation on the part of the black artist so that "our (white?) hostilities" will "vanish." In short, this identification of white thinking and white feeling with "human unity" allows Howells to associate mankind with being white, and thus to delimit physical and spiritual blackness.

What this meant, of course, was that, as within the dominant literary establishment itself, the African-American text would need to adopt certain literary "universals" in order to obtain recognition. These universals were grounded in a language of white aesthetic conventions and, more importantly, in white perceptions and ultimate distortions of black experience. As a result, they nearly rendered invisible any uninhibitied articulation of black experience beyond those shared by the dominant group. Black critics in later years went so far as to indirectly refute Howells by basing their criticism upon "blackness"; as did James Weldon Johnson when he wrote in his *Book of American Negro Poetry*:

> Dunbar was of unmixed Negro blood; so, as the greatest figure in literature which the colored race in the United States has produced, he stands as an example at once refuting and confounding those who wish to believe that whatever extraordinary ability an Aframerican shows is due to an admixture of white blood" (36).

It should be noted, however, that within their own literary exile, blacks did indeed maintain their own mutual visibility through the creation and perpetuation of an oral tradition of slave narratives and songs. And while even in this realm, the dominant group periodically raided portions of the black oral tradition (particularly the songs), and further insured black invisibility, black oral tradition during post-bellum flourished unabated and eventually was adopted and incorporated by the 1920's writers of the Harlem Renaissance.

Oral narratives and songs spoke of alienation and frustration in black people's search for freedom and equality which, for many black writers, began in the quest for cultural literacy. To discover the word was not only a means to potential economic advancement for black people, but also a way for black artists to know and sustain some kind of cultural identity. This quest for literacy was especially important when blacks of the early 20th century began migrating in large numbers from the rural south to northern cities. Estranged from a rural folk consciousness, black writers, such as Jean Toomer, Langston Hughes, and Zora Neale Hurston, began to experiment with the embedment of folktales, plantation songs, and religious chants in their writings.

With this quest for cultural identity, however, came also the critical stricture that black literature should only continue the repudiative mind-set of the oral narrative so long as it had some primary political function. That is, black critics, such as W.E.B. DuBois and Alain Locke, insisted that all black creative writing promote race-pride; as DuBois put it in the essay, "Negro Art," "Negro art is today plowing a difficult row. We want everything that is said about us to tell of the best and highest and noblest in us." (55).

But in adhering to this nationalistic principle, the black writer was constricted into developing mere social commentary for the betterment of black life. And while in light of continued racial injustice, this stance seemed timely, it also valorized message while ignoring the value of form and technique. So much so that even ambiguity or irony in language came to be viewed with suspicion and an impediment to the realities of black life. It was what DuBois called "the social compulsion" of black literature. He maintained that the African-American text should have its foundations in "the sorrow and strain inherent in American slavery, on the difficulties that sprang from emancipation, on the feelings of revenge, despair, aspiration, and hatred which arose as the Negro struggled and fought his way upward" (53). Therefore, as Gates comments, "the critic became social reformer, and literature became an instrument for the social and ethical betterment of the black man" (56). As a result, black literature often failed to capture the sublimity and poignancy that both form and content could convey. Language became merely a medium in which statements could be clearly expressed.

The critical emphasis of content over form surfaced repeatedly in black criticism throughout the 20th century, and was especially intense in the writings of Richard Wright, James Baldwin, Ralph Ellison, and an assortment of critics known as The Black Aestheticians. While the Harlem Renaissance nationalists, in emphasizing message, sought to underscore the distinctiveness of their culture, Richard Wright took a more reactionary stance. Believing as he said in his essay, "Blueprint for Negro Writing," that "a nationalistic spirit in Negro writing [should carry] the highest possible pitch of social consciousness" (338), Wright's "message" would be culled in what thereafter would be known as the protest tradition in black criticism and literature.

Like most literary movements, Wright was clearly and strongly reacting against previous black writers and critics whom he saw as being "dressed in knee pants of servility, curtseying to show that the Negro was not inferior, that he was human, and that he had a gift comparable to other men" (333). Wright believed that black literature should realistically portray the realities of black oppression in what he saw as their outsider status within a brutal and unjust environment. In addition, as Ralph Ellison comments in his "Richard Wright's Blues," Wright felt that blacks "could reject the [oppressive] situation, adopt a criminal attitude and carry on an unceasing psychological scrimmage with the whites, which often flared forth into physical violence" (94).

Wright's medium of scrimmage was, of course, his many writings, chief of which was his 1940 novel, *Native Son*; a novel which has since been considered both a prototype for and a detriment to the African-American text.   For instance, Eldridge Cleaver thought that "of all black American novelists, and indeed of all American novelists of any hue, Richard Wright reign[ed] supreme for his profound political, economic, and social references" (105); whereas James Baldwin commented that because *Native Son*'s protagonist, Bigger Thomas, was presented as a violence-prone and therefore "subhuman" black, the character ultimately represented "the failure of the protest novel [because it lied] in its rejection of life, the human being, the denial of his beauty, dread, power, in its insistence that it is this categorization alone which is real and which cannot be transcended" (23).   But regardless of *Native Son*'s critical status, the arguments for or against the novel never moved it beyond the confines of political/social commentary.   Furthermore, while devaluing form and remaining mired in message, black critics, from the 1940's onward, continued to reproduce similar reductionist strictures and literary conventions of the dominant literary establishment.

Wright's own recognition of the dominant literary culture extended itself to his endorsement of literary convention particularly in later years when he softened his militancy and adopted a more integrationist posture. Wright, in his 1957 essay, "The Literature of the Negro of the United States," argued that black literature would become indistinct from mainstream literature: "At the present moment there is no more dominant note in Negro literary expression. As the Negro merges into the mainstream of American life, there might result actually a disappearance of the Negro as such" (227-28).

One example of Wright's desire "to merge into the mainstream," appears in his review of Zora Neale Hurston's *Their Eyes Were Watching God*. Wright states that "Miss Hurston seems to have no desire whatever to move in the direction of serious fiction. . . . The sensory sweep of her novel carries no theme, no message, no thought" (25). His observation not only ignores the relativity of "serious fiction" but also underscores a central premise in black literary production. In making his demands for theme and message and thus adhering to conventional aesthetics, Wright helped to assure that any African-American text could escape repression if it conformed to what was commonly (and in some circles remains) the dominant society's set of critical expectations. Thus Wright can be subsumed in a typical and accommodational reading as, for instance, Phyllis Rauch Klotman gives when she writes of Wright:

> The [black] outsider, for example, is a victim of the twentieth-century ethos which has instilled in him anonymity, facelessness . . . [and who is] able to choose outsideness as a way of life with the opportunity to build an identity, a self apart from the identity forced upon him by society" (63).

Clearly Klotman places Wright's work in the critical tradition of say a Hemingway or a Steinbeck or to put it another way, absolutism of content and form reduce the African-American text to cultural as well as literary indistinction. Of course indistinction may seem a necessary trade-off considering the times and influences of Richard Wright, James Baldwin, or any other black writer/critic who seeks recognition, and in the process reproduces conventions and stereotypes of the dominant group. But what of those texts which remain suppressed; texts which find no (white) audience; and in particular a text such as Hurston's *Their Eyes Were Watching God*? Hurston's work, after all, was all but forgotten during the ensuing years of such writers and critics as Wright, Baldwin, Ellison, or the Black Aestheticians of the 1960's.

Lorraine Bethel maintains that "black woman writers have consistently rejected the falsification of their Black/female experience, thereby avoiding the negative stereotypes such falsification has often created in the white American female and Black male literary traditions" (177). To Bethel this includes "Richard Wright's *Native Son* [which] is one example of how the falsification of the Black experience for the purpose of political protest can result in characters that reinforce racist stereotypes" (187). Similarly, June Jordan designates Wright's *Native Son* as the prototype of a black protest novel and Hurston's *Their Eyes Were Watching God* as the prototype of a novel of presumably authentic black affirmation, and she also argues that "the function of protest and affirmation are not, ultimately, distinct: that . . . affirmation of Black values and lifestyles within the American context is, indeed, an act of protest" (6).

Jordan's and Bethel's arguments for authenticity and affirmation raise a pertinent question: Why would "protest" be valorized instead of "affirmation"? In the criticism of the African-American text, certainly the issue of sexism cannot be ignored as a primary reason for the suppression of Hurston's work, but let us look first at the critical significance of protest versus affirmation, specifically as it relates to mid-20th century literary criticism.

In his "Blueprint for Negro Writing," Richard Wright wrote that,

with the gradual decline of the moral authority of the Negro church, and with the increasing irresolution which is paralyzing the Negro middleclass leadership, a new role is developing upon the Negro writer. He is being called upon to do no less than create values by which his race is to struggle, live, and die. (330)

For Wright, the artist had become a redeemer who would lead his people out of the wilderness of disenfranchisement, just as a century before black religion had contrived and propelled the dream for a "land of Canaan."

If we accept Bethel's determination, Wright's values led to a falsification or, perhaps more precisely, a denial of any positive aspects of black life because, like a religious believer, Wright looked instead to an eventual utopian world where blacks had overcome their oppression and repression. And since the ideological impetus for Renaissance nationalists and Wright's "protest" was a reproduction of the decidedly Western notions of active development and linear movement, affirmation, based as it often is on insular sustentation, did not fit largely into their ideology.

By the end of the 1940's, however, some black critics, such as William Gardener Smith, began to complain that "too often . . . in Negro novels do we witness the dull procession of crime after crime against the Negro. . . . These chronicles of offenses . . . do not constitute art" (199). And with the emergence of James Baldwin and Ralph Ellison, black criticism took a distinct turn away from the protest tradition. It was a shift which, although momentarily disrupted by the Black Aestheticians of the 1960's, would open out the rigid mindset of black criticism and signal the reconstruction of the African-American text.

Baldwin argued that protest writing merely confirmed society's view of its social problems and did not therefore offer what he believed should be a redemptive context for the individual. For Baldwin the business of the writer was to reveal what it meant to be a human being without regard to either black or white America.

Undoubtedly, Baldwin did not move black criticism much beyond a content analysis reminiscent of Howells' original criticism and, in addition, seemed only to reaffirm the continuing reproduction of an American literary tradition which, like Klotman's analysis, posited the individual challenge and eventual transcendence of society. But if in some respects Baldwin still remained subsumed in Western literary tradition, he was nonetheless determined to take the African-

American text out of the public realm of overtly propagandistic discourse. In *No Name in the Street*, Baldwin writes that "these two [the artist and the revolutionary] seemed doomed to stand forever at an odd and rather uncomfortable angle to each other, and they both stand at a sharp and not always comfortable angle to the people they both, in their different fashions, hope to serve" (172).

The writer, Baldwin believed, could not surrender herself, or her creativity, to public discourse. The writer existing as she does in a private sphere was only concerned with the individual in society and therefore could only give credence and affirmation to the dignity and sanctity of individual life. Thus, while Baldwin clearly sets himself inside the 20th century Western tradition of writers as isolate, his writings nonetheless represent a shift in black criticism by affirming that change can only come from within the self and not as the result of any external literary or socio-political strictures.

Like Baldwin, Ralph Ellison gave affirmation to the importance of selfhood and transcendence, but he also stressed that black folklore should be raised to the level of art in order for the African-American text to achieve its most intrinsic meanings. For Ellison, the black folk speaker or singer provided some sense of continuity to the chaos of the slave experience. As with all folklore, black folk tradition had a classically-based function of being both delightful and instructive but it also provided slaves with some sense of communal consciousness, and in the place of physical freedom, gave distinction to their lives.

Ellison writes in *Shadow and Act* that "Negro folklore, evolving within a larger culture which regarded it as inferior, was an especially courageous expression. It announced the Negro's willingness to trust his reality, rather than allow his masters to define these crucial matters for him" (173). Furthermore, Ellison contended that, like their precursors, 20th century blacks survived because they remained conscious of their folk traditions in church, in song, and in children's tales. Thus Ellison believed that black folklore was the richest source for the black writer because it served to affirm both "the humor as well as the horror of our living" (80).

In all fairness to Richard Wright, Ellison thought Wright's earlier work (*Uncle Tom's Children*) contained many vital elements of folklore which, as Robert G. O'Meally points out, "emerged not from overt Marxist or Kierkegaardian theorizing [as with *Native Son*], but from the fiction itself, which was rich in folklore" (158). O'Meally's comments, however, represent a significant point of departure in our discussion of Ellison principally because, like Baldwin, Ellison wished to go beyond Wright's later ideological impositions, and stressed instead the value of a writer's individual expression in search for her own "metaphysical perspective":

> If the Negro, or any other writer, is going to do what is expected of him he's lost the battle before he takes the field. . . . For us the question should be, What are the specific forms of [black] humanity, and what in our background is worth preserving or abandoning? The clue to this can be found in folklore. . . . (169-71)

The use of folklore in *Invisible Man* not only presents a more capacious reflection of black life, but also intensifies the creative tension of Ellison's prose. Sermons and sermon-like speeches, allusions to blues and gospel songs and lyrics, and various uses of the "dozens" and signifying games in dialogue all transform *Invisible Man* from a simple social referent into what the African-American text or any literary work can become, and that is, a system of signs that make a particular aesthetic unity of form and content. This unity compels the reader to confront a distinctly African-American world-view that, like the slave folk tradition, allows the text and its reader to engage in the subjective "freedom" to repudiate both social and literary repression.

In other ways, of course, *Invisible Man* is accommodational in that it replicates the dominant culture's myth of the rugged individual. But while both Ellison and Baldwin, in moving the African-American text out of its "protest" mode, opted for a traditionally thematic approach to literature, they succeeded for a time in opening out new possibilities for the African-American text. The Black Aestheticians, on the other hand, shifted its critical emphasis back to "political beliefs" and thus back to content-centered criticism as the only mode of critical and literary production for the African-American text.

The Black Aestheticians' socio-political ideology had its roots in the Harlem Renaissance nationalists and was clearly a reflection of the turbulent 60's. But unlike the Renaissance nationalists, the Black Aestheticians were deterministic in the extreme and insisted, as Maulana Ron Karenga dictated in his "Black Cultural Nationalism," "that all Black art, irregardless of any technical requirements . . . must be functional, collective and committing [and] must expose the enemy, praise the people and support the revolution" (33). These neo-nationalists produced a decade or so of literature and especially poetry which was used to preach a manifesto of both nationalism and revolution. In a 1975 interview, the poet Ted Joans called them the "hand-grenade" poets (6) who closely followed Addison Gayle's own ideological premise for black literary production:

> To evaluate the life and culture of black people, it is necessary that one live the black experience in a world where substance is more important than form, where the social takes precedence over the aesthetic, where each act, gesture, and movement is political, and where continual rebellion separates the insane from the sane, the robot from the revolutionary. (xi-xii)

Gayle's call for "substance" over "form" is fraught with contradiction because, like his Harlem Renaissance progenitors, Gayle falls into the similar stratagem of deterministic analysis, and finally into a kind of universality: "The archetypal hero of the twentieth century," Gayle writes, "is the black man evidencing, in his daily struggles, the universal of characteristics—hope, love, determination, and courage" (280). Gayle's substantive criticism is reminiscent of and seems only to invert Howell's critique by replacing "white thinking" with "black thinking," as if consciousness were predetermined by color alone. Gayle correctly observes that this "doctrine . . . was impossible to arrive at before black men [and women?] moved to reclaim their history" (280). But what doctrine have "they" arrived at? Is it not a decision that once again merely reproduces a deterministic and narrowly thematic view of literature?

In making their literary value judgments, the Black Aestheticians had once again internalized standards of the dominant group, and in doing so, had brought their criticism to an exhausted full circle. The irony of this normative criticism in the midst of socio-political revolution was not lost on contemporary black writers of the 60's and 70's. For instance, Ntozake Shange observes in her poem, "takin a solo. . ," that "we assume a musical solo is a personal statement, we think the poet is speakin for the world. There's something wrong there, a writer's first commitment is to the piece, itself. How the words fall & leap/or if they dawdle & sit down fannin themselves" (10). Or in another instance, Ishmael Reed writes in his satirical novel, *Yellow Back Radio Broke Down*:

> What's you beef with me Bo Shmo, what if I write circuses? No one says a novel has to be one thing. It can be anything it wants to be, a vaudeville show, the six o'clock news, the mumbling of wild men saddled by demons. (36).

No longer were black writers willing to align themselves beside the prescriptive ghosts of Howells or Bigger Thomas; instead they resisted the strictures of the Black Aestheticians and sought to recontinue the aesthetic reunification that Ellison had initiated in the 1950's. And thus, as John M. Reilly states, they began to "move into the realm of conscious history not directly through the advancement of political program but first through the reconstruction of their unique materials: the language, technique, and genres of literary art" (6).

Unlike Ellison, however, these emerging writers choose to work in a cultural context that is perhaps more indigenous to black life. While they may draw from the tradition of black folklore or from traditional literary themes, their fiction also stresses a communal consciousness. Each writer creates a particular black community that instead of defining itself in relation to external ideology or to the dominant group, emphasizes its own past, its own forms, and within this context it is significant to note that this "new" fiction is produced largely by black women.

Having freed themselves of a particular ideological and literary repression, such contemporary writers as Alice Walker and Toni Morrison have transformed the African-American text into a limitless medium of discovery and affirmation. As a result, black literary studies, after being for so long tied to overtly sociology and political ideology, is now beginning to recognize that it must, as Henry-Louis Gates states, "direct [its] attention to the nature of black figurative language, to the nature of black narrative forms. . . , [and] to the fundamental unity and form of content" (68). But while black criticism has entered this present mode, it is black women writers themselves who have been chiefly responsible for redefining and reaffirming the African-American text.

Chapter II

Cultural Reconstruction in the African-American Text

To more fully understand how contemporary black women writers have reshaped and redefined the African-American text, we must look to the narratives of earlier black women writers and to the socio-historical forces which shaped their narratives and their world-views.

"The Black Woman," according to Joyce Ladner, "suffers from the twin burden of being Black and female" (227). It is a double jeopardy which has haunted, tormented, and also, paradoxically, liberated black women, or as Ladner writes, "we have always been 'free,' and able to develop as individuals even under the most harsh circumstances" (274). Beginning in slavery, the black woman, unlike the male-protected and pedestalled white woman, was forced, since she could never be protected by her male, slave counterpart, to develop into a mature, self-reliant being; she was the first, truly liberated American woman.

It goes without saying, however, that, as Ladner's "free" suggests, the autonomous or liberated position of slave women could in no way suggest that black women lived fully meaningful lives. Both male and female slaves were beasts of burden, seen as sub-human by their white masters, relegated to drudges in an accursed economic system. But the "double jeopardy" of female slaves involved more than the unenviable status of working animal; she was also the object of brutal and perverse desire.

As Frances Beale writes:

Her physical image has been maliciously maligned; she has been sexually molested and abused by the white colonizer; she has suffered the worst kind of economic exploitation, has been forced to serve as the white woman's maid and wet nurse for white offspring while her own children were more often than not starving and neglected. (92)

This "depth of degradation," as Beale says, "to be socially manipulated [and] physically raped" (92) has had a lasting impact on the real lives and literary images of black American women. That black women survived and flourished under these conditions is surely a testament to the human spirit, but that is precisely the point: Black women, in the midst of both racism and sexism, did survive, and their ability to do so was the glue that bound together black communities both during and after slavery.

In oral narratives and songs, the black woman was accurately depicted as cook, housekeeper, nursemaid, seamstress. The stereotyped "mammy" also appeared in black narratives as a nurturing, mother figure who cared for and held together the fragile bonds of her family while at the same time she was a surrogate mother for the master's children. It should be noted, however, that while the "mammy" in white narratives was often depicted as the wise but obedient surrogate mother, the mammy in black oral tradition, according to Barbara Christian in her *Black Feminist Criticism*, "kicked, fought, connived, plotted, most often covertly, to throw off the chains of bondage" (5) and to protect her children who were brought and sold at will.

During post-bellum, black women continued these dual roles of both nurturer and worker. Since the black male could neither actively nor aggresssively compete with his white counterparts, black women had no alternative but to support their families in such positions as lowly cooks and housemaids to white employers. Nonetheless, black women provided a stabilizing force for their families and thus their communities in that their dual roles inside and outside the black community ensured its continued social and economic survival.

But as Elizabeth Higgenbotham maintains, "Even though many Black women [were] able to overcome difficult situations, Black women [were] not 'super-women' devoid of needs and emotions" (96). The black woman, as the grandmother says in Zora Neale Hurston's *Their Eyes Were Watching God*, "[was] de mule uh de world so fur as Ah can see" (29). In spite of her active role in family and community, or perhaps because of it, black women were continually seen by American society at large as, if one will permit the paradox, dominant nonentities.   Black males, unable to assert themselves as productive members of society, felt their masculinity debased not only by white males but also and ironically by black females who were often the sole breadwinners in the white man's kitchen.   At the same time, white society saw black women as mere chattel, performing what were considered neither "ladylike" tasks nor significant economic contributions to society.

According to bell hooks, "a devaluation of black womanhood occurred as a result of the sexual exploitation of black women during slavery that has not altered in the course of a hundred years" (53).   During 19th-century patriarchal America, a "good" woman was pure, sexually repressed and physically fragile; she was married, a mother, or a spinster who was dependent on and, therefore, nonthreatening to men.   The "bad" woman was dirty, promiscuous, physically and mentally strong; she was a prostitute, a laborer, a single mother who paid her own way in spite of her social and political invisibility. Black women more so than white were often subjugated to such positions and thus, as a continuation of slavery's institutional rape, "a myth was created," according to Gerda Lerner, "that all black women were eager for sexual exploits, voluntarily 'loose' in their morals and, therefore, deserving none of the consideration and respect granted white women" (44).

In attempting to dispel this myth, middle-class black women would internalize white values of feminine decorum; in short, they tried to become "ladies." But both white men and women resisted such change which became, as hooks asserts, "a calculated method of social control" (60). In this social order, black women remained on the bottom, hidden behind the stereotypes of either the "mammy" or the "sapphire," subordinated by a patriarchy in both white and black society, and economically exploited in a capitalist system.   Within this maligned and constricted context, black women began to write.

Beginning with Francis E. W. Harper's novel, *Iola Leroy, or Shadows Uplifted* (1892), women writers attempted to combat the negative stereotypes of black women. Since 19th-century black writers were writing almost exclusively to white audiences, women writers sought to accommodate white audiences by softening the preceived myth of black women as lacking in femininity. The literary establishment and white readership required that the female heroine be physically beautiful, chaste, well-bred, and above all, white; therefore, black women writers, in order to gain recognition, had no choice but to create a character who possessed these attributes in addition to "passing" for white. In doing so, they hoped to dispel the anti-feminine myths and thus "uplift" the black race by showing that black women were, quite simply, complex human beings who could, like white heroines, experience joys and sorrows. Easily appropriated by the white race, these early novels created the genteel tradition of the tragic mulatta.

Harper's Iola is the beautiful, well-educated daughter of a wealthy plantation owner and a quadroon. In brief, the novel exposes the brutality of slavery particularly in regard to the widespread rape of black women by white men, and thus much of the novel depicts Iola's attempts to resist white men and consequently retain her virtue. Unfortunately, black writers, in their efforts to combat stereotypes, created their own stereotype of the tragic mulatta which, as a literary convention, persisted well into the 20th century. Nella Larsen's *Passing* (1929) and Jessie Fauset's *The Chinaberry Tree* (1931) are two later examples of novels which had as their central character the tragic mulatta.

Like *Iola LeRoy*, *Passing* and *The Chinaberry Tree* depict heroines whose loyalties are necessarily divided between black and white social codes. That these heroines continued to exhibit white, middle-class values was perhaps indicative of the Harlem Renaissance writer's need to prove black feminine respectability. Nonetheless, as Barbara Christian points out, "the [women's] literature had yet to catch up with the new reality" of black women who were not, as the mulatta novels depicted, "genteel ladies whose conflicts about color and class tended to be closer to fairytale than anyone's imagined or factual reality" (8).

Many black women by the 1920's had migrated North and taken employment that was oftentimes more oppressive than in the South. They were domestics, factory workers, and prostitutes whose lives were submerged in stereotypes and who witnessed their fragile Southern heritage being blasted apart by an urban, industrial society. In light of this continued devaluation, some black writers, such as Langston Hughes, saw a need to preserve that complex and genuine heritage in a representative literature:

> [The common folks] furnish a wealth of colorful, distinctive material for any artist because they still hold their own individuality in the face of American standardizations. And perhaps these common people will give to the world its truly great Negro artist, the one who is not afraid to be [herself]. (260)

The common people did find their artist in the voice of Zora Neale Hurston. Hurston's writing represents a transition from the stereotyped mulatta figure to more varied and complex characters which were drawn from Hurston's own background. She, perhaps more than any other post-Harlem Renaissance writer, was adamant in her desire to portray black people as they realistically appeared to her. Born and raised in the all-black town of Eatonville, Florida, Hurston's short stories, novels, and collected folklore captured the tones, gestures, expressions, and traditions of the common folk.

Hurston's novel, *Their Eyes Were Watching God* (1937), is now regarded by many black women writers and critics as one of the great American novels of the 20th century. Her life and work are experiencing their own renaissance primarily because of the immeasurable influence they have had on contemporary black women writers. For example, Alice Walker writes in her edited edition of *A Zora Neale Hurston Reader*:

> Reading *Their Eyes Were Watching God* for perhaps the eleventh time, I am still amazed that Hurston wrote it in seven weeks; that it speaks to me as no novel past or present, has ever done, and that the language of the characters, that "comical nigger 'dialect'" that has been laughed at,

denied, ignored, or "improved" so that white folks and educated black folks can understand it, is simply beautiful. There is enough self-love in that one book — love of community, culture, traditions — to restore a world or create a new one. (2)

In light of recent civil rights and feminist movements, black women writers, critics, and feminists look to and are inspired by Hurston for her courage in "being herself" and resisting the patriarchal and literary bonds in American society. Hindered by the "double jeopardy" of color and sex, Hurston had to beg publishers to consider her work even after becoming a well-known writer, but to her credit, she continued to produce a considerable amount of work between 1934 and 1960 in spite of the prevailing social and literary impediments.

This attempted suppression of Hurston's novel, however, involved much more than race and sex. She was also a victim of a dominant culture and a literary establishment which could not appropriate her work. Since much of fiction was written, as Walker says, in "nigger dialect" and also celebrated the folk traditions of black community, the dominant culture found it, unlike the mulatta novels, difficult, if not impossible, to acept as "serious fiction." Ironically, black critics, too, found Hurston's work unpalatable for similar reasons. Richard Wright maintains, "Miss Hurston voluntarily continues in her novel [*Their Eyes Were Watching God*] the tradition which was forced upon the Negro in the theater, that is, the minstrel technique that makes the 'white folks' laugh" (25). Black critics also ridiculed Hurston for her "failure" to show the exploitation and oppression of blacks; she portrayed characters who were often unconcerned about political or social issues; they lived their lives and conducted their relationships as a community of people might do; but critics, like Sterling Brown, found that her "pastoral" renderings of Southern black life were "shadowed by squalor, poverty, disease, violence, enforced ignorance, and exploitation" (Washington 16), which, to their dismay, Hurston chose to ignore. She did so because she did not believe in reducing the whole of black experience to racism and exploitation. In her controversial essay, "How It Feels to Be Colored Me," she writes:

But I am not tragically colored. There is no great sorrow damned up in my soul, nor lurking behind my eyes. I do not mind at all. I do not belong to the sobbing school of Negrohood who hold that nature somehow has given them a low-down dirty deal and whose feelings are hurt about it. Even in the helter-skelter skirmish that is my life, I have seen that the world is to the strong regardless of a little pigmentation more or less. No, I do not weep at a little pigmentation more or less. No, I do not weep at the world—I am too busy sharpening my oyster knife. (153)

This is not to say that Hurston did not recognize nor succumb to racism or discrimination; surely Hurston's life is a testament to how an independent black woman can be cruelly and brutally maligned by society. And in her later years, Hurston would sadly learn that "the strong" remained the male-dominanted radical/racial protest school of black litera- ture which seemed to believe that oppression was indeed the sum total of black lives. But her essay does reflect her insistence on writing literature that realistically portrays black experience; or, as June Jordan comments, "Black people do not represent issues: they represent their own, particular selves in a Family/Community setting. . . that fosters the natural, person-postures. . ." (6).

This emphasis upon community and familial concerns is what, I think, has renewed Hurston's appeal for contemporary black women writers and critics. No longer restricted by the zeitgeist of protest/propagandistic criticism and literature and spurred on by the feminist movement, contemporary black women writers find in Hurston's fiction and collected folklore the sense that literature can and should more fully represent the whole of black life and experience, and consequently can do more to reaffirm and celebrate black culture than any protest/political black literature can ever do. In sum, Hurston shifted the emphasis from the "problem" of being economi- cally and psychologically crippled to emphasizing the inherent strengths and weaknesses of black people and in doing so revealed a totality of black reality.

Hurston's most celebrated novel, *Their Eyes Were Watching God*, reflects this totality of black reality by countering the real and literary stereotypes of black women. Furthermore, *Their Eyes Were Watchng God* represents not only a foundation for a black female literary tradition but also presents a textual basis for black feminist criticism.

In the rural South of Hurston's youth, black people commonly sought community, identity, and emotional support in their own oral, musical, and visual expressions and narratives. *Their Eyes Were Watching God* reflects this folk bonding and centers it specifically in the language and expressions of a self-affirming black female retrospective as it is retold by the heroine of the novel. The novel opens with this sign of affirmation:

> Now, women forget all those things they don't want to remember, and remember everything they don't want to forget. The dream is the truth. Then they act and do things accordingly. (9)

Janie Wood's childhood begins as an illusionary dream. She is a "yaller girl" whose mother was raped by a white schoolteacher and "'took to drinkin' likker and stayin' out nights'" (37). Deserted by her mother, Janie lives with Nanny, her grandmother, who works for some "'quality white folks up dere in West Florida'" (20). Janie plays with white children, wearing their second-hand clothing, "'which still wuz better'n what de rest uh de colored chillun had'" (22), and never realizing until she is six that she herself is black. The pragmatic Nanny shelters Janie from the vicissitudes of life and is determined to give Janie a materially better life than either she or Janie's mother ever had. Janie dreams about love and thinks she finds her dream in Johnny Taylor, a man whom Nanny calls a "'trashy nigger'" (27). Responding to Janie's impulse to individuality, Nanny tries to protect her by convincing her to marry Logan Killicks, a middle-aged farm owner; she wants Janie to "pick from a higher bush and sweeter berry" (28). But Nanny's protectiveness has ironic overtones because while she insists that Janie have a better life, she also condemns her to live her life as an object of both possession and desire. In short, she wants Janie to conform to the racial and sexual milieu which surrounds her:

> "Honey, de white man is de ruler of everything as fur as Ah been able tuh find out. Maybe it's some place way off in de ocean where de black man is in power, but we don't know nothing but what we see. So de white man throw down de load and tell de nigger man tuh pick it up.

> He pick it up because he have to, but he don't tote it. He hand it to his womenfolks. De nigger woman is de mule uh de world so fur as Ah can see. Ah been prayin' fur it tuh be different wid you. Lawd, Lawd, Lawd!" (29)

For the remainder of the novel, Janie struggles against conforming to this condition of black women, and in doing so, Hurston moves the black woman beyond stereotype as Janie slowly establishes her own identity and her desired place within the community.   In submitting to an arranged marriage, Janie "extend[s] herself outside of her dream" (26) of love and individiality; and her dream becomes further subordinated as Killicks begins to treat her more and more like a vacuous automaton, telling her, "'You ain't got no particular place. It's whenever ah need yuh'" (52).

As she tires of her "protected" life, Janie yearns again for her dream of love and identity. She believes she finds that dream when she meets and marries Joe Stark, a strong-willed, self-righteous entrepreneur who becomes the mayor of his own town. But while Janie leads a more comfortable life with Joe, she remains no freer since she continues to be protected from experiencing life. Joe places her on his own pedestal requiring that, as the mayor's wife, she not associate with nor participate in the games and conversations of the common folk. Furthermore, he belittles her whenever she does not conform to his vision of what a wife should be: "'she is uh woman and her place is in de home'" (69). "So gradually, she press[es] her teeth together and learn[s] to hush" (111), but after nearly 20 years of marriage and subservience, Janie begins to rebel. At this point, the stereotypes start to disintegrate as Janie begins to find her voice:

> "Sometimes God gits familiar wid us womenfolks too and talks His inside business. He told me how surprised He was 'bout y'all turning out so smart after Him makin' yuh different; and how surprised y'all is goin' tuh be if you ever find out you don't know half as much 'bout us as you think you do. It's so easy to make yo'self out God Almighty when you ain't got nothing tuh strain against but women and chickens." (117)

In recognizing the reasons for her unhappy marriage, Janie feels compelled to defiantly break free from her patriarchal bonds and inwardly return to her dream for identity and place.   After Joe's death, Janie feels no compunction to remarry; she merely continues to work in Joe's country store while fending off any potential suitors.   One day, however, Vergible "Tea Cake" Woods saunters into the store and after some polite conversation asks if Janie would like to play checkers.   This is a significant scene in the novel because no one has ever asked her to participate in any kind of social activity: "Somebody wanted her to play.   Somebody thought it natural for her to play.   That was even nice" (146).

Janie steps off her socially/sexually prescribed pedestal and perceives in Tea Cake the renewal of her dream: she finds someone who treats her as an equal partner and thus empowers her to "'to partake wid everything'" (186), including the opportunity to "listen and laugh and even talk some herself if she wanted to.   She got so she could tell big stories herself from listening to the rest" (200).   Both go to the Everglades as migrant workers; they work side-by-side picking beans and tomatoes and participating in the songs and dances of the migrant community.

But Hurston's story does not end "happily ever after"; while Tea Cake as her lover and partner brings simple joys to Janie's life, he is also the source of destructiveness in the novel and points to a continuation of the novel's male/female conflicts. Tea Cake becomes involved in a series of fist- and knife-fights; he slaps Janie "to show he [is] boss" (218); and he also takes two hundred dollars from her without her permission.   In the end, Janie is forced to kill the man she loves.

Thus, unlike the literary tradition of women's abandonment or death for the sake of love, Hurston inverts her novel's resolution; Janie remains the survivor and, as such, she returns to her grandmother's home secure in her own identity and place; and perhaps most important, is able to perpetuate her vision by communicating it to the community.   In doing so, *Their Eyes Were Watching God* becomes a story within a story. Janie tells her retrospective to her close friend, Pheoby, as a means of transmitting and affirming her experience of self-discovery and survival and thereby enlightening Pheoby who afterwards says, "'Ah done growed ten feet higher from jus' listenin' tuh you, Janie. Ah ain't satisfied with mahself no mo'"" (284). Also, by embedding her experience within the black tradition of oral story-telling, she gives to Pheoby, and thus to the reader, a more varied and complex vision of herself and of her world and also demonstrates the kind of solidarity and bonding that has been essential in maintaining black women's identity and survival.

As the novel demonstrates, Janie's own self-affirming ritual becomes a source of inspiration and strength to her friend, but, in addition, she also encourages Pheoby to tell others in the community in hopes of perpetuating her oral legacy: "'You can tell 'em what Ah say if you wants to. Dat's just de same as me 'cause mah tongue is in mah friend's mouf: (17). Thus Janie "breaks the barriers" of stereotype and invisibility for others as she herself has thrown off her own false images. And in celebrating this antithesis to the real oppression of black women, *Their Eyes Were Watching God* anticipates and encapsulates a comparable renaissance of contemporary black women's literature and criticism which encompasses what Lorraine Bethel calls "black women-identification":

> . . . the basis of Black feminism and Black feminist literary criticism . . . is most simply the idea of Black women seeking their own identity and defining themselves through bonding on various levels—psychic, intellectual, and emotional, as well as physical—with other Black women. . . . Black women-identification is Black women not accepting male—including Black male—definitions of femaleness or Black womanhood. . . . (184).

Contemporary black women writers such as Alice Walker and Toni Morrison have drawn from Hurston's vision and redefined the African-American test in ways which reflect this "women-identification." One way, in particular, in which this is done is by depicting women not as Wright's or Ellison's traditional black outsiders, who themselves conform to the mythic American tradition of self reliance and individualism, but as integral members of their communities; her quest for self and place, then, becomes not only an internal one, but also encompasses her family and community surrounding her. Consequently, black female contemporary novels reflect a more balanced view of black people and culture by presenting the multiplicities of daily living; as Toni Morrison commented in an interview with Robert B. Stepto: "Frequently, what I [find] so lacking in most black writing by men. . . is a sense of joy, in addition to oppression and being a woman or black or whatever" (485).

This sense of "joy" and/or sorrow, this sense of a fully realized depiction of black women and black communities stems from a communal tradition which Chikwenye Okonjo Ogunyemi calls "womanism." Ogunyemi in the essay, "Womanism: The Dynamics of the Contemporary Black Female Novel in English," maintains that the black woman writer does not concentrate solely upon "analyzing" or "attacking" patriarchy as some white women writers. Alienated and isolated from the "real world power" (69) of white patriarchy, black women writers choose instead to concern themselves with a kind of domesticity "that celebrates black roots, the ideals of black life, while giving a balanced presentation of black womanhood" (72). It is not that black women writers do not acknowledge their victimization by a white and black patriarchy or that they are not dehumanized by racism, sexism, and poverty, but unlike white women who, by comparison, "[write] from a position of power" (69), black women writers cannot within the present "world power structure" (69) assume the same stance. Womanists must therefore seek a literary position that is primarily inspirational wherein "its wholesome, its religious grounding in black togetherness, is [their] gospel of hope" (79).

In contemporary novels, black female characters look to themselves, to their relationships, and to their communities for strength and growth; and along with the traditions of oral narratives, the "blues," and familial ties, black women writers present, as Ogunyemi states, the ideal "for black unity where every black person has a modicum of power and so can be a 'brother' or 'sister' or a 'father' or a 'mother' to the other" (72). And thus, black women writers seek not to necessarily devalue or usurp black social structures, but to enhance them.

Taking into account this vision for both "personal and collective identity" must, of course, present its own mediating position. To underscore the viciousness of racism and sexism, contemporary writers may create female characters who, in striving for some sense of identity and autonomy, become isolated by community members who wish to uphold a standard of normality which serves to keep black women in a secondary and thus an invisible position. For example, in Alice Walker's *The Color Purple*, the main character, Celie, is forced both physically and emotionally into a position of subservience and isolation. She transcends her invisibility first by writing letters, in her own oral dialect, to God and later to her sister; and then she meets Shug, the dance-hall singer, who introduces her to the blues, and to a society which affirms the need for black togetherness. Thus, in the midst of their isolation from both the white and black mainstream communities, Celie and Shug create their own meaningful, "womanistic" community.

Black women writers may also show that a reversal can occur when black female characters create their own sense of alienation by succumbing to what soon becomes a distorted reality; it is the untenable desire to conform to white, middle-class social and economic values, and to internalize what it means to be beautiful and therefore worthy in white society that frustrates and eventually incapacitates black characters to the degree that their sense of identification becomes distorted. This distortion is central to Toni Morrison's *The Bluest Eye*. Bombarded and humiliated by images of white beauty and bourgeois ideals, Morrison's characters lose themselves to self-hatred and mutual ostracism until their lives cease to have any meaning beyond seeking the unattainable—to be white. They become, then, not only alienated from their heritage, but also from who they really are, and eventually, like the child Pecola who yearns for blue eyes, have no recourse save for madness. As Morrison explains in an interview with Jane Bakerman, "I want, here, to talk about how painful consequences are of distortion, of love that isn't fructified, is held in, not expressed" (60). It is this absence of self-love and self-worth which separates Morrison's characters from their traditions; and in the absence of such communal coherence and kinship ties, her characters in *The Bluest Eye* have little impetus to survive and grow.

But from whatever stance black women choose to write, we are presented with a vision that affirms the need for wholeness. "How to survive whole," Morrison continues, "in a world where we are all of us, in some measure, victims of something" (60) is the paramount issue in contemporary black women's literature; and while it carries on the rectifying tradition of the African-American text, it more importantly represents a progression from past literary and critical movements. As we shall see in Morrison's fiction, we can no longer delimit the African-American text to stereotypes and singlular ideologies. In her novels, we witness a diversity of black women's (and men's) experience in America which cannot be reduced to simple critical strictures and which, by its very form and content, refutes those same strictures. It is a search for a fully realized self and place within the community; it is a search for "the dream [that] is the truth."

Chapter III

The Bluest Eye:
Selfhood and Community

Toni Morrison's first novel, *The Bluest Eye* (1970), opens with a sample of the idyllic "Dick and Jane" primer. The primer acts as an ironic frame for the entire novel's narrative; its sanitized image pervades all of American society — from schoolbooks to print and electronic media — as the standard for family behavior and beauty:

Here is the house. It is green and white. It has a red door. It is very pretty. Here is the family. Mother, Father, Dick, Jane live in the green-and-white house. They are very happy. See Jane. She has a red dress. She wants to play. Who will play with Jane? See the cat. It goes meow-meow. Come and play. Come play with Jane. The kitten will not play. See Mother. Mother is very nice. Mother, will you play with Jane? Mother laughs. Laugh, Mother, laugh. See Father. He is big and strong. Father, will you play with Jane? Father is smiling. Smile, Father, smile. See the dog. Bowwow goes the dog. Do you want to play with Jane? See the dog run. Run, dog, run. Look, look. Here comes a friend. The friend will play with Jane. They will play a good game. Play, Jane, play. (7).

This primer prose is immediately repeated two more times; a second time it is printed at a more accelerated speed, the words running together without punctuation:

Here is the house it is green and white it has a red door it is very pretty here is the family mother father dick and jane live in the green-and-white house they are very happy see jane she has a red dress she wants to play who will play with jane (7)

A third time the pace is frenzied:

Hereisthehouseitisgreenandwhiteithasareddooritisveryprettyhereisthef
amilymotherfatherdickandjaneliveinthegreenandwhitehousetheyarever
yhappyseejaneshehasareddressshewantstoplaywhowillplaywithjane (8)

The reader is confronted with this dizzying visual impression and compelled to mediate between the familiar simplicity of the childhood version and the chaos of second and third versions. Each chapter is prefaced by fragments of the frenzied prose in order to continually remind the reader of the undeniable contrast between this pervasive white, middle-class myth and the tragic desolation of the novel's central character, Pecola Breedlove and her family, who are incapable of attaining this dream myth.

But as we continue to read, the initial presence of the children's prose also assumes further significance as a guide-post to the novel's complex structure. Embedded within the prose are the novel's three levels of narrative consciousness: the first level is the personal, idealized consciousness of child-hood, as demonstrated by Pecola's yearning for blue eyes; the second represents the less sedate, less naive consciousness of the novel's central narrator, Claudia McTeer, who, as an adult, recalls the ambivalence that the idyllic prose's image creates; the third version provides the social/historical consciousness of an objective narrator who, by repeating the prose and exposing the contrast between the ideal and the real, offers the reader no escape from her anger at the dissolution of black lives.

In the first chapter, Claudia's narrative retrospective of her childhood describes a world where "adults do not talk to us—they give us directions. They issue orders without providing information" (12). We are immersed in Claudia's reckoning of her childhood; we see through the eyes of a child, but it is not nor can it be a fully accurate account. Her reminiscences are split between a child's and an adult's viewpoint, and thus she vacillates from a personal subjectivity to an objective recognition that serves to emphasize the difficulty in sorting through her feelings for herself, her friends, for her world around her, and for what those feelings and impressions meant then and now.

"But was it really like that?" (14), Claudia's adult voice asks herself as she recalls her mother's extreme anger at her catching a cold. Or perhaps did her mother's anger mask a deeper concern and love for Claudia: "So when I think autumn, I think of somebody with hands who does not want me to die" (14). Claudia's modulating voice requires the reader to answer these and other questions that elude her; but, as we shall see, the answers cannot be (nor should they be) arrived at easily or concretely, and the complexity of the novel's narrative consciousness contributes to this indeterminacy.

Barbara Christian comments, in her "A Promise Song," that Pecola's story does not follow "the usual mythic [cycle] of birth, death, and rebirth, from planting to harvest to planting. Hers will proceed from pathos to tragedy and finally madness" (140). Neither are we given a linear structure wherein the novel begins at the beginning. Instead, the first section, "Autumn," tells us the whole of Pecola's story and a portion of Claudia's on the introductory page, as Claudia makes the analogy to her and her sister Frieda's failed planting of marigold seeds:

> We had dropped our seeds in our own little plot of black dirt just as Pecola's father had dropped his seeds in his own plot of black dirt. Our innocence and faith were no more productive than his lust or despair. What is clear now is that of all of that hope, fear, lust, love, and grief, nothing remains but Pecola and the unyielding earth. Cholly Breedlove [Pecola's father] is dead; our innocence too. The seeds shriveled and died; her baby too. (9)

Claudia makes it clear at the outset that she now knows as an adult that she cannot valorize a particular emotion; she will only, as she says, "take refuge in how" (9) Pecola's tragedy and madness have come to be. And so she implicitly asks the reader to suspend the certitude of value judgments — and for good reason. Linear order and mythic coherency provide illusionary moments in the narratives of life, in nature, as well as in fiction. Neither in life nor in nature can we consistently take comfort in certitude; both can be uncompromising and unpredictable; both will defy the narrative illusions, those moments of "innocence and faith" that we create for them. And while these illusionary moments may provide a survivalist mechanism, such survival and sustentation are devoid of authenticity, of an embraceable culture within which a community may clearly and positively identify and develop itself.

In the first chapter of "Autumn," Claudia establishes the time, place, and structure of the novel and introduces us to some of the players of the story. She also acquaints the reader with a community in turmoil, and by doing so, produces yet another of the novel's structural masterstrokes. Claudia's hints of conflict are told with the typical child's voice of ironic innocence and nonchalence, and as her fragmentary accounts of abuse and their resultant effects weave in and out of her narrative, they reflect the confusion and conflict within the community that in turn leaves the reader both puzzled and vaguely horrified. We fleetingly learn that Mr. Henry ["our roomer" (14)], has committed some unspeakable act. We also know "that old Dog Breedlove," a moniker clearly instilled by Mrs. McTeer, "[has] burned up his house, gone upside his wife's head, is [now] in jail, and everybody, as a result, [is] outdoors" (17, 19). The "everybody" includes "Mrs. Breedlove, [who is] staying with the woman she work[s] for; the boy, Sammy, [who is] with some other family" (19); and Pecola, who has been taken in by the McTeers, because she is "a girl who has no place to go" (17).

Pecola's initial appearance signals a shift to a more coherent narration, although still told by Claudia with the subjective naivete of a child. We come to know Pecola's idealized consciousness, and significantly we learn of her object of desire and the symbolic perpetrator for the central conflict and incongruity in the novel:

> Frieda brought her four graham crackers on a saucer and some milk in a blue-and-white Shirley Temple cup. She was a long time with the milk, and gazed fondly at the silhouette of Shirley Temple's dimpled face. Frieda and [Pecola] had a loving conversation about how cu-ute Shirley Temple was. (19)

Like the Dick and Jane primer, Frieda and especially Pecola are attracted to the order and perfection of this manufactured image; it is an image that connotes myriad, contrived values including how a girl and/or woman should look, act, and even feel.

Considering Pecola's pathetic circumstances, it is understandable perhaps that she be drawn to an idealized fabrication, and as readers, we fully sympathize with Pecola when she is scolded by Mrs. McTeer for drinking three quarts of milk in one day. Claudia says that Pecola ". . . took every opportunity to drink milk out of it just to handle and see sweet Shirley's face" (22). But her extreme fondness for the cup also represents an indictment against the whole of a value system that has afflicted not only Pecola and her family, but an entire community. Both Frieda and Claudia, whose parents, unlike Pecola's, have provided a relatively loving and stable family environment, are themselves drawn to what Shirley Temple represents.

At first, Claudia is envious of Shirley Temple because, as she says, "she danced with Bojangles, who was *my* friend, *my* uncle, *my* daddy, and who ought to have been soft-shoeing it and chuckling with me." Later her envy turns to hatred and inspires her to tear apart the "blue-eyed Baby Doll[s]" (19) that she receives for Christmas. Even as a child, she senses, as Cynthia Davis points out, "the force of alien cultural images. She [knows] that white 'ideals' deny her reality by forcing it into strange forms of appearance and experience." But Claudia, too, learns to introject those "ideals" knowing that, in order to be loved and accepted, she must conform because, as she remembers, "all the world had agreed that a blue-eyed, yellow-haired, pink-skinned doll was what every girl child treasured" (20).

There is a gentle irony in Claudia's ambivalent "adjustment." As a child, she cannot fully know the locus for her conversion; she changes for the sake of unfettered love; she, as Susan Willis puts it, "perceive[s] the world . . . prior to the advent of capitalism and bourgeois society" (37). But in the duality of both partial recognition and later submergence,

Claudia establishes for herself and for the reader an empathic link to Pecola's extreme seduction, and thus for the remainder of the novel, Claudia's sometimes child, sometimes adult voice attempts to make sense of an entire community's fragmentation. To further open out Claudia's wavering perceptions and to delineate the social milieu surrounding her narrative of Pecola and the Breedlove family, Morrison offers in the remaining chapters a distanced narration that serves to answer why a cultural reification occurred in the community.

The Breedlove family lives in "an abandoned store on the southeast corner of Broadway and Thirty-fifth Street in Lorain, Ohio" (30). The narrator's sparse and subdued description of the Breedlove home is analogous to the emptiness and despair of their domestic life, particularly in the almost anthropomorphic characterization of their furniture:

> The furniture had aged without ever having become familiar. People had owned it, but never known it. No one had lost a penny or a brooch under the cushions of either sofa. . . . No one had given birth in one of the beds—or remembered with fondness the peeled paint places. . . . No young girl had stared at the tiny [artificial] Christmas tree and remembered when she had decorated it, or wondered if that blue ball was going to hold, or if HE would ever come back to see it.
> There were no memories among those pieces. Certainly no memories to be cherished. (31-32)

Unlike the seeming stability of the McTeer household, the Breedlove furniture reflects the emotional stasis in their lives; they live a futile, makeshift existence, rootless, and devoid of affirmative values or traditions. And like a kind of spatial blues, even the dialogue—a call and response between Cholly and a delivery man about a defective sofa-accentuates their futile and oppressive existence:

> "Looka here, buddy. It was OK when I put it on the truck. The store can't do anything about it once it's on the truck."
> "But I don't want no tore couch if'n it's bought new."
> "Tough shit, buddy. Your tough shit. . . ." (32)

The Breedloves are victims of a racist, class conscious society that has forced them to live unnatural lives; but while their lives have been battered by racism's more tangible effects of extreme poverty and deprivation, the most insidious effects of racism as well as sexism are represented by the maliciousness of stereotypes. Claudia explains that although the Breedloves' ". . . poverty was traditional and stultifying, it was not unique. But their ugliness was unique." And it is unique because the Breedloves have fully internalized their ugliness; Claudia remembers that "it was as though some mysterious all-knowing master had given each one a cloak of ugliness to wear, and they had each accepted it without question." Their "all-knowing master" is, of course, a dominant culture that has pervasively imposed their white, male-engendered stereotypes upon them; as Claudia continues:

> The master has said, "You are ugly people." They had looked at themselves and saw nothing to contradict the statement; saw, in fact, support for it leaning at them from every billboard, every movie, every glance. "Yes," they had said. "You are right." And they took the ugliness in their hands, threw it as a mantle over them, and went about the world with it. (34)

But while the tragedy of Pecola and her family results in their loss of self-worth, it more significantly becomes the catalyst for the abuse and violence that the family inflicts upon each other and that is further inflicted upon them by a community who themselves are caught up in the same futile cycle of desire and denigration.

We are introduced to this pattern of infliction in what appears to be a typical morning scene in the Breedlove household. Pauline cajoles her sleeping, drunken husband into getting coal and lighting their cold stove. His recalcitrant response precipitates a violent argument between them replete with punching, kicking, and screaming. The narrator comments that these "quarrels" give "substance" to their lives. Their mutual abuse is reminiscent of scenes from earlier black novels such as Bigger's murder of his girlfriend, Bessie, in *Native Son* or Lutie's self-defensive murder of Boots in Ann Petry's *The Street*. And indeed, like those novels, the closeness between Cholly and Pauline necessitates that they abuse one another in an attempt to displace their pent-up, inarticulated fury toward a hostile world; and thus they become mutual scapegoats who assuage their inadequacies by assuming positions of tenuous dominance.

But Morrison is not intent upon merely affirming the existence of the fear, frustration, and fury inherent in black life; she wishes to expose the psychic causes for the social distortions within a black community. To do so, Morrison has chosen Pecola as her thematic representative; but in other seemingly unrelated episodes and scenes about various members of the community, she reminds the reader that the individual, the personal story, reveals but one product of a larger, more complex, more diffused social and herstorical schema.

Pecola, during these scenes of parental bedlam, wishes to make herself "disappear" (39). But Pecola cannot escape her loveless home anymore than she can hide from a community which shuns her for her inherited ugliness, even though she vainly tries: "Each night, without fail, she pray[s] for blue eyes" and "she [is] not without hope. To have something as wonderful as that happen [will] take a long, long time" (40). She does, however, disrupt her reverie long enough to wonder why she is shunned: "Long hours she sat looking in the mirror, trying to discover the secret of the ugliness . . . that made her ignored or despised at school, by teachers and classmates alike" (39).

Her wonderment clues the reader to the prescriptional nature of her "ugliness"; its secret is ensconced in a cultural construct for what constitutes beauty. The narrator tells us, in the novel's only concrete description of Pecola's facial features, that "her teeth [are] good, and at least her nose [is] not big and flat like some of those who were thought so cute" (40). Where, then, does Pecola's ugliness reside? Like the deeply dark and equally ostrasized Emma Lou in Wallace Thurman's *The Blacker the Berry*, Pecola is "ignored and despised" not only because of her bitter, indigent parents, but because she is, as the "high-yellow dream children" (52) call her, "black and ugly black e mos" (61).

Pecola is victimized by the community's hierarchy of color and caste. It is, of course, founded upon the white model for beauty, but it has undergone a necessary modification: those members who appear more white are accorded preference over those who are not. Within the socio-historical context of black oppression, appearances have always been tantamount to gaining approval from the dominant group, however illusionary those appearances or approvals may be. Consequently, those who are able to mimic white social codes may hope to move socially and economically in both the black and white worlds, and thus, color serves to determine class order. Or as Claudia says, those children who are most white are prized by parents and teachers alike (61), which is in accordance with this wholly internalized 20th century color and caste mind-set. The double jeopardy of being both poor and "ugly" excludes Pecola, or any equally "ugly" male or female, from sharing in whatever social or economic tidbits that may be offered. Moreover, neither Pecola nor her parents can fully comprehend the depth of their ostracism, and therefore are further denied the power to perspicaciously modify their positions.

To fully understand why the Breedloves are powerless to change and why the community has so little regard for them requires that the narrative shift abruptly in order to bridge the gap between individual experience and social history. From "Autumn," the novel shifts to "Winter," and the chapters therein detail the cold, sterile undercurrents within the community. It is a relatively new Northern black neighborhood which, in its physical and psychic disengagement from the South, is attempting to reestablish some reified social order. But their basis for continuity patterns a white, bourgeois social model that, for Morrison, denies all "passion[s]" and "human emotions" (68) in black life. The narrator recalls the urban black woman's adaptive development with scathing description:

> They go to land-grant colleges, normal schools, and learn how to do the white man's work with refinement: home economics to prepare his food; teacher education to instruct black children in obedience; music to soothe the weary master and entertain his blunted soul. Here they learn the rest of the lesson begun in those soft houses with porch swings and pots of bleeding heart: how to behave. The careful development of thrift, patience, high morals, and good manners. In short, how to get rid of the funkiness. The dreadful funkiness of passions, the

funkiness of nature, the funkiness of the wide range of human emotions.

Wherever it erupts, this Funk, they wipe it away; where it crusts, they dissolve it; whenever it drips, flowers, or clings, they find it and fight it until it dies. They fight this battle all the way to the grave. The laugh that is a little too loud; the enunciation a little too round; the gesture a little too generous. They hold their behind in for fear of a sway too free; when they wear lipstick, they never cover the entire mouth for fear of lips too thick, and they worry, worry, worry about the edges of their hair. (68).

In this passage Morrison laments the lack of sensuality and spontaneity in the lives of these dispossessed, Northern black women. It accentuates the emotional void which has been precipitated by the tremendous influence of the white, social model. Implied within her lament, in the denial of "this Funk" is an alternative social code that, within the novel's context, has been repressed. This alternative code is encompassed within the historically enriched social theories of Bethel's "woman-identification" and Ogunyeimi's "womanism" which, for Morrison, translates into what she calls the "neighborhood"; as she tells Robert Stepto:

And there was this life-giving, very, very strong sustenance that people got from the neighborhood. One lives, really, not so much in your house as you do outside of it, within the 'compounds,' within the village, or whatever it is. (474)

But in the explicit neighborhood of *The Bluest Eye* there lives instead "one such girl from Mobile . . . who [does] not sweat in her armpits nor between her thighs, who smell[s] of wood vanilla. . . . Her name [is] Geraldine" (70-71). Geraldine, her husband, Louis, and her son, Louis Junior, are, as Geraldine tells her son, "colored people"; and she explains to him the difference between "colored people" and "niggers": "They were easily identifiable. Colored people were neat and quiet; niggers were dirty and loud" (71). In Geraldine we see the status quo personified; she embodies the community's strictly codified caste system; and into this "compound" wanders Pecola who is positioned here as both an oppositional and connective force within the novel. She represents all that Geraldine and her community's commodified value system abhor, while at the same time her movement within the community serves to more clearly define the community's alienation, repression, and internalization.

This oppositional move appears to pit the pure evil of Geraldine against the poor helplessness of Pecola. Pecola meets Louis, Jr., at the playground, and Louis invites Pecola into his home. Pecola is enthralled by its interior: "How beautiful, she thought, What a beautiful house." But once inside, Louis Jr. throws a black cat in her face," and afterwards he swings it around his head. The cat is thrown against the window and killed just as Geraldine enters the house. Predictably, Louis accuses Pecola of killing the pet, and Geraldine sides with her son telling Pecola to leave her house. Clearly in this scene Pecola embodies all that Geraldine despises and fears:

> She had seen this little girl all of her life. Hanging out of windows over saloons in Mobile, crawling over the porches of shotgun houses on the edges of town, sitting in bus stations holding paper bags and crying to mothers who kept saying "Shet up!" Hair uncombed, dresses falling apart, shoes untied and caked with dirt. They had stared at her with great uncomprehending eyes. Eyes that questioned nothing and asked everything. Unblinking and unabashed, they stared up at her. The end of the world lay in their eyes, and the beginning, and all the waste in between. (75)

This emotionally wrenching scene cannot but move the reader to fully sympathize with Pecola, who, as she is frightened from the house, "[can]not hold [her head] low enough to avoid seeing the snowflakes falling and dying on the pavement" (76). But the hatred we may feel for Geraldine and Louis, Jr., is tempered by our knowledge that they, too, are victims. They all represent "products" of a commodified system that, in its imposition of social and economic order through the manufactured image, seeks to and succeeds in inverting the truth of their lives; and by doing so, the system causes each character to uneasily mediate between the contradictions of image and substance, and thus between the divisiveness of desire and self-hatred.

Morrison's strategy of inversion is further reflected in the next section of the novel. "Spring," a mythic time for rebirth and renewal, begins not with images of optimism and growth, but with images of agony and frustration. Claudia speaks of spring as an analogy to child whippings: ". . . these long twigs . . . made us long for the steady stroke of a strap or the firm but honest slap of a hairbrush" (78). She also hears her mother sing "about trains and Arkansas," which conjures up visions of a more innocent time and place. And finally, when Claudia finds her sister "crying [a] tired, whimpering cry," she learns that Mr. Henry, the boarder, has "touched" Frieda's "tiny breasts," and that "Daddy" has "beat him up" and driven him from their home (78). This inversion of a father-figure who molests children is complemented by the inverted figure of Pecola's mother who denies her child love and showers it instead upon a white child.

Claudia and Frieda follow Pecola to her mother's workplace in a home in a white neighborhood. When Pecola accidentally smashes a fresh-baked berry cobbler onto the kitchen floor and splatters the white child's new pink dress, Pauline knocks Pecola to the floor, and thereafter consoles the white child as if she were her own. Like Geraldine, Pauline, too, treats Pecola as a pariah. Juxtaposed against the clean, white home and the "pink and yellow girl" (87), Pauline's own child reminds her of the shabby reality of her present life; and at this juncture in the novel, the scene serves as a fitting preface to an extended narrative of Pauline's life.

Perhaps the most significant portion of *The Bluest Eyes* is Pauline Breedlove's chapter. Encompassed in Polly's life is the whole of the Northern community's alienation and dissonance. And since her story is told in the voice of a distanced narrator as well as in the voice of Pauline's own dialect, we are privy to both her way of perceiving her world in its distinctive colors and images and to a narrator's expansion upon what Pauline, in her subjective position, is incapable of understanding. From her beginnings in Alabama and later in Kentucky, Pauline has been plagued by a "crooked, archless foot that flop[s] when she walk[s]." Like the deformities of Sherwood Anderson's small town grotesques, Pauline's physical deformity leaves her burdened with a sense of ". . . separateness and unworthiness," and yet like the *Winesburg, Ohio* characters, she possesses a sensitive nature which compells her to long for consistency and purpose in her life:

> Restricted, as a child, to this cocoon of her family's spinning, she culti-
> vated quiet and private pleasures. She liked, most of all, to arrange
> things. To line things up in rows—jars on shelves at canning, peach
> pits on the step, sticks, stones, leaves. . . . She missed—without knowing
> what she missed—paints and crayons. (88-89)

Pauline's youth recalls Alice Walker's "grandmothers" in her essay, "Our Mother's Garden," whose lives were "driven to a numb and bleeding madness by springs of creativity in them for which there was no release" (233). In her youthful privacy and freedom of imagination, Pauline is still able to cultivate her "springs of creativity." When she first sees Cholly, she describes the encounter as an artist arranging colors:

> When I first seed Cholly, I want you to know it was like all the bits of
> color from that time down home when all us chil'ren went berry
> picking after a funeral and I put some in the pocket of my Sunday
> dress, and they mashed up and stained my hips. My whole dress was
> messed with purple, and it never did wash out. Not the dress nor me. I
> could feel that purple deep inside me. And that lemonade Mama used
> to make when Pap came in out the fields. It be cool and yellowish, with
> seeds floating near the bottom. And that streak of green them june
> bugs made on the trees the night we left from down home. All of them
> colors was in me. Just sitting there. So when Cholly came up and
> tickled my foot, it was like them berries, that lemonade, them streaks of
> green the june bugs made, all come together. . . . (92)

But when she and Cholly marry and move north to Lorain, Pauline's creative sensitivity, like the "grandmothers'" before her, is thwarted by a new form of enslavement. Her countrified ways, her need for quietude and privacy, are not in keeping with a paradoxically impersonal yet public urban setting. She remembers that "Northern colored folk was different too. Dicty-like. No better than whites for meanness. They could make you feel just as no-count, 'cept I didn't expect it from them" (93).

During the days when Cholly is working in the steel mill, Pauline is left alone and bored; her neighbors are "amused by her because she [does] not straighten her hair. . . . Their goading glances and private snickers at her way of talking (saying 'chil'ren') and dressing develop[s] in her a desire for new clothes." And thus, both Pauline and Cholly begin to feel the community's social pressure to conform; it is a pressure which only serves to tear them apart because they can measure up to neither each other's nor to the community's expectations. "The sad thing was," as the narrator recounts, "Pauline did not really care for clothes and makeup. She merely wanted other women to cast favorable glances her way" (94). Pauline is awash in hopeful naiveté, and coupled with her loneliness and boredom, she finds an outlet for her repressed creativity by replacing her youthful orderliness with the "perfection" of Hollywood's silver screen, and eventually turning with a vengeance against all those who, to her, represent imperfection.

The narrator tells us that "there in the dark her memory [is] refreshed and she succumb[s] to her earlier dreams." Pauline's dreams include not only the romantic love that she experienced with Cholly, but more importantly, she is ". . . introduced to another — physical beauty." The movies inspire her to equate "physical beauty with virtue" (97); she finds a world without flaws, a sense of wholeness which she cannot know in real life. Like the rest of her community, Pauline has begun the process of attempting to internalize images and their implied values.

She and the marginalized community succumb to what Jean-Paul Sartre calls "the Look." According to Sartre, one's reality and identity are both confirmed and threatened by "the Look of the Other," the Other, in this instance, constituting the gaze of white media images: "I grasp the Other's look at the very center of my act as the solidification and alienation of my own possibilities." To think of oneself as an individual is to exist in a world of potentialities, but one remains subjected to the gaze of the Other as an object in another's perception: "The Other as a look is only that — my transcendence transcended" (239). If one can appropriate the Other in one's own world, one can therefore transcend it: "Thus, my project of recovering myself is fundamentally a project of absorbing the Other" (340).

One is then left in a position of vacillation; the individual will attempt to control the potential self while at the same time relying upon the Other's look to confirm one's identity. Pauline's self-contempt rests between this vacillation of self and Other; she can neither realize the potentialities of self nor adequately confirm her identity in a conscious appropriation of the Other. Thus, she tries consciously to reject her potential self as well as "the Look of the Other":

> "There I was, five months pregnant, trying to look like Jean Harlow, and a front tooth gone. Everything went then. Look like I just didn't care no more after that. I let my hair go back, plaited it up, and settled down to just being ugly." (98)

But Pauline's withdrawal from the conflict only serves as a means to escape responsibility to define herself; and her acquiescence further enables the look of the white society to continue its permeating gaze. She along with the black neighborhood become frozen into an unnatural position of what Frederic Jameson in *Marxism and Form* calls a "we-object" subjected to the continual gaze of a "Third":

> It is only when I feel myself become an object along with someone else under the look of such a "third" that I experience my being as a "we-object"; for then, in our mutual interdependency, in our shame and rage, our beings are somehow mingled in the eye of the onlooker for whom we are both somehow "the same": two representatives of a class or a species, two anonymous types of something. . . . (249)

In light of this exacerbatingly coercive gaze, it seems reasonable that the marginal group in its communal vulnerability would "choose" to become objects in order to minimize their isolation and alienation because, as Claudia remembers, "being a minority in both caste and class, we moved about the hem of life, struggling to consolidate our weaknesses and hang on, or to creep singly up into the major folds of the garment" (18).

For Geraldine, this means the emulation of a "perfect" bourgeois existence; for Pauline, it means an escape into a facade of religious righteousness, "holding Cholly as a model of sin and failure . . . [and] bore[ing] him like a crown of thorns, and her children like a cross." She also has ". . . the good fortune to find a permanent job in the home of a well-to-do [white] family . . . ," whose members treat her with "affection" (100), and enable her to evade the disorder or aberration in her life and to collaborate with "the Look of the Other":

> Here she could arrange things, clean things, line things up in neat rows. . . . Here she found beauty, order, cleanliness, and praise. . . . Pauline kept this order, this beauty, for herself, a private world, and never introduced it into her storefront, or to her children. (101-102)

Instead, Pauline instills in them a fear of all that is in opposition to her adopted beauty and order:

> Them she bent toward respectability, and in so doing taught them fear: fear of being clumsy, fear of being like their father, fear of not being loved by God, fear of madness like Cholly's mother's. Into her son she beat a loud desire to run away, and into her daughter she beat a fear of growing up, fear of other people, fear of life. (102)

Even though Pauline sometimes thinks about "the old days" (102), the days when she possessed the stirrings of a self-sustaining creative vision, it is the inverted quality of her life that has left its mark on the children. By allying herself with the gaze of the Other and denying the inadequacy and imperfection of her and her family's existence, Pauline instills into Pecola all that she fears and hates in herself, and therefore, in her own distorted way, she "teaches" Pecola how to survive their status of cultural invisibility.

Pauline's biography/autobiography, coming as it does at the approximate center of the novel, provides a nucleus around which the whole of the text revolves: Her private life revealed is emblematic of the public tragedy of one community's inability and/or unwillingness to recognize themselves. And to further underscore the inverted quality of "Spring," Pauline's narrative of loss and self-denial ironically recedes with images of Christian rebirth, which is the ultimate form of cultural assuagement: "'My Maker will take care of me. I know He will. Besides, it don't make no difference about this old earth. There is sure to be a glory" (104).

The dissonance of Pauline's chapter blend irrevocably into "Spring's" next-to-last chapter wherein Cholly Breedlove's life is explored. His last name is quite obviously ironic because love is not nor has it ever been what he breeds. Instead, his life is a compilation of abandonment, self-contempt, circuitousness, and despair. In his one move toward what he preceives as a positive act, Cholly attempts to "save" his daughter and himself from their lives of pain and contradiction. That he chooses to do so by raping Pecola is horrifically yet inexorably symptomatic of still another one of the novel's characters whose life has been culturally mutilated.

Cholly's life encompasses cycles of birth and rebirth, of love and hate, all of which, in accordance with the novel's design, are immediately inverted into states of unnaturalness. He is deserted by his father at birth and by his mother when he is only four days old. His Great Aunt Jimmy rescues him from a junk heap and raises him, although she neglects to inspire him with direction or education. In some ways, Cholly's life assumes a familiar literary position; he is "black boy" in Wright's autobiography; he is Ellison's "invisible man." But unlike those individual narratives, Cholly's life carries with it no overtly political or reformist trademarks; his vision is, out of necessity, grounded in a narcissism which has at its center his desire for external "perceptions and appetites": "Abandoned in a junk heap by his mother, rejected for a crap game by his father, there was nothing more to lose. He was alone with his own perceptions and appetites, and they alone interested him" (126).

When Aunt Jimmy dies, Cholly is again "abandoned" but he experiences another "rebirth" in his first sexual encounter. On the day of Aunt Jimmy's funeral, Cholly runs off with Darlene to make love in the woods. This mythic scene of initiation is undercut, however, by the intrusion of two white men who shine their flashlight on the two lovers and goad Cholly into "performing" for them; and as he does, his hatred grows not for the white men but for Darlene because,

> . . . he hated the one who had created the situation, the one who bore witness to his failure, his impotence. The one whom he had not been

able to protect, to spare, to cover from the round moon glow of the flashlight. (119)

Under the gaze of the Other, Cholly learns early in life that survival in his unnatural state of being a "we-object," is predicated upon his collaboration with the Other, and thus he makes the black woman the object of his displaced fury. Moreover, when Cholly thinks that Darlene might be pregnant, his hatred for her compels him to repeat his father's cycle of abandonment; he runs away to Macon to look for him, but the cycle is completed when he finds his father and is rejected by him. With nothing left to lose, Cholly thus becomes "dangerously free": "Free to feel whatever he felt — fear, guilt, pity. Free to be tender or violent, to whistle or weep. Free to sleep in doorways or between the white sheets of a singing woman" (125).

Cholly becomes the first of Morrison's various travelling black male characters whom she valorizes in various interviews and in later novels. They are drawn from the rich, American literary tradition of the "Running Man," who, as Phyllis Klotman states, ". . . rejects the values of the culture or society in which he finds himself by birth, compulsion, or volition, and literally takes flight" (3). The danger in Cholly's free-flight, however, is made apparent when, in his "god-like state," he marries Pauline and is confronted with "the constantness, varietylessness, the sheer weight of sameness [which drives] him to despair and [freezes] his imagination." While his sense of freedom permits him to retreat from the gaze of the Other and from the inherent self-contempt of being a "we-object," his usefulness in motion has never been predicated upon human connectedness. He is therefore "rendered . . . totally disfunctional" (126) by not only the "sameness" and routine, but also by a total lack of social adroitness:

> Having no idea of how to raise children, and having never watched any parent raise himself, he could not even comprehend what such a relationship should be. Had he been interested in the accumulation of things, he could have thought of them as his material heirs; had he needed to prove himself to some nameless 'others,' he could have wanted them to excel in his own image and for his own sake. Had he not been alone in the world since he was thirteen, knowing only a

dying old woman who felt responsible for him, but whose age, sex, and interests were so remote from his own, he might have felt a stable connection between himself and the children. As it was, he reacted to them, and his reactions were based on what he felt at the moment. (126-127)

The narrator's presentation of Cholly's social ineptitude and malformation is reflected in the relative brevity of Cholly's chapter, and while it may be inordinately hyperbolic, it serves to intensify the ensuing moral ambiguity in Cholly's violation of his daughter. But more significantly, the passage points to an increasingly prominent characteristic in the text. Save for Cholly's violation, there are no scenes in the novel which depict any meaningful interaction between Cholly and his children. He is thus made conspicuous by his absence and, in fact, so too are all of the male characters in the novel. When they do appear, they serve as sexual agents and/or precipitators of fear, hate, or madness. Ironically, their very absence serves to accentuate their unrelenting power because on the few occasions when they do surface, it is to deny presence to the female and to remind her that she is subservient to their Look in a patriarchal society.

In the hope of defending themselves against this denial, the novel's female characters try to collaborate with and internalize the desired Look of the Other, and ultimately they please and placate their male-centered society. In the end, they must seek placation by external means; in the white baby dolls and in the white men's homes; in the mimicry of white men's values and in reified lifestyles. Pecola, on the other hand, has no concrete means with which to defend herself. Instead, she holds on tight to her illusion that blue eyes will bring her love and acceptance. Cholly, in literally elevating himself at the expense of his daughter, fully appropriates her presence, drives her into madness, and in so doing, frees Pecola from any further need for defense.

But only a reductive reading could assign a wholly individuated blame to Cholly or to any of the male characters. Undeniably, as Madonna M. Miner states, "when Cholly rapes his daughter, he commits a sacrilege—not only against Pecola, but against her vision of love and its potential" (188). And in part, as Miner continues, the rape of Pecola,

> . . . contributes to a much larger woman's myth, which tells of denial and disintegration, which unveils the oft-concealed connections between male reason, speech, presence and female madness, silence, absence. (188)

Miner, however, fails to recognize and examine the cultural distortions within the text that lead up to the rape scene's final moment of "denial and disintegration." Certainly there are oppositionally "connective" forces at work in the novel; and certainly Cholly's disgraceful act has left Pecola bereft of presence and fully silenced into madness. But these two characters do not function in either a spatial or emotional vacuum within the text; Morrison wants the reader to equally see why Cholly has entered into this unforgiveable act.

Miner reasons, and rightly so, that Cholly's desire for Pecola is intermingled with his desperate desire to rekindle his earlier happiness with Pauline and to ". . . regain an earlier perception of himself as young, carefree, and whimsical by using this girl/woman as medium" (180). But however indelicate it may seem in this instance, there is selfishness in any act of giving, and giving is indeed what Cholly thinks he is doing. As Pecola washes dishes in the kitchen, Cholly looks at her "young, helpless presence" and wonders:

> What could he do for her—ever? What give her? What say to her? What could a burnt-out black man say to the hunched back of his eleven-year-old daughter. . . . How dare she love him? Hadn't she any sense at all? What was he supposed to do about that? Return it? How? What could his calloused hands produce to make her smile? What of his knowledge of the world and of life could be useful to her? What could his heavy arms and befuddled brain accomplish that would earn him his own respect, that would in turn allow him to accept her love? (127)

Cholly chooses to physically give of himself because it is all that he has left to give, and in his state of bewildered and besotted despair, he is all that he is capable of giving to Pecola. That is why the rape scene appears as it does at the very end of Cholly's chapter. We see throughout the chapter the gradual dissolution of Cholly's life, and thus in addition to the complexity of his emotions, we cannot fail to recognize that his act, however repugnant, is born out of his own desperate sense of invisibility. "Father" Breedlove, from birth, has been locked away from a culture and a neighborhood which prizes and aspires to the myth of the Dick and Jane primer. He is the one character who has had no opportunity to achieve purpose—however illusionary it may be—save for his one pathetic act; he has been "assigned" a mere function given to him by his neighborhood and by a "Third"; and in keeping with his function, he cannot, regardless of whether he senses freedom or bondage, overcome his assignation: He is an "ugly nigger." He is "Dog Breedlove."

Cholly's rape of Pecola is a culminating gesture in the novel's strategy of inversion. For Cholly, the cycle of love-hatred—from Darlene to Pauline to Pecola—seems to be completed. As Claudia remembers at the beginning of the novel:

> . . . there were no marigolds in the fall of 1941. We thought, at the time, that it was because Pecola was having her father's baby that the marigolds did not grow. A little examination and much less melancholy would have proved to us that our seeds were not the only ones that did not sprout; nobody's did. (9)

As Claudia now understands it, nature, events, and characters within her story have gone completely awry; there remains neither natural nor human growth; love does not grow; identities remain malformed and misshapen. But for Pecola, the cycle has begun anew. She must live with the consequential burden of the act, and as a means to relief and to a potential rebirth, she turns once again to her illusion and ultimately finds it "realized" in the spiritual source of Soaphead Church.

In the last chapter of this false spring, the narrator introduces us to one final character in the novel. Pecola turns to Soaphead, a "Spiritualist and Psychic Reader" (137), to grant her wish for blue eyes. Soaphead is a West Indian of "mixed blood" (132) whose schoolmaster father was dedicated to preserving their "rapidly fraying [British] gentility" (135). Soaphead's rigid, socially conscious upbringing inhibits him from tolerating any display of chaos, "any hint of disorder and

decay" (134).   But he also recognizes the narrowness in his
acculturated upbringing, and thus, unlike the destructive self-
hatred of Pauline or Cholly, Soaphead is able to intellectualize
the pain and despair and he tries to remove himself from the
fray by cultivating misanthropy.   He finds comfort in a different kind of illusion.   It is a "reality" formed through language:
"Knowing his label provided him with both comfort and
courage, he believed that to name an evil was to neutralize if
not annihilate it" (130).

When Pecola comes to Soaphead, he clearly recognizes her
requisite: "Here was an ugly little girl asking for beauty." He
names and understands the "evil" incongruity, and so it is, for
him, a "logical petition":

> Of all the wishes people had brought him — money, love, revenge — this
> seemed to him the most poignant and the one most deserving of
> fulfillment.   A little black girl who wanted to rise up out of the pit of
> her blackness and see the world with blue eyes. (137)

White beauty, white living, white "freedom:—these are what
the characters in *The Bluest Eyes* long for, strive for, and yet can
never realize.   "For the first time [Soaphead] honestly wish[es]
he [can] work miracles" (137), so much so that he vows to
"annihilate" the evil by, like Cholly, assuming his own god-like
stance.   To prove to Pecola that she can indeed have blue eyes,
Soaphead uses a dying, old dog as a catalyst for her conversion.   Like Junior's helpless cat, Pecola is once again made
analogous with the defenseless animal as scapegoat.   Soaphead
tells Pecola to feed the dog his food (mixed with poison) and
tells her that if "'. . . nothing happens, you know that God has
refused you.   If the animal behaves strangely, your wish will
be granted on the day following this one'" (138).

Of course, the dog convulses and dies, and Pecola is left with
her illusion of blue eyes.   Soaphead, like all the principal male
characters, has again selfishly denied presence to Pecola, but
his own act of appropriation has gone one step further; he
composes a letter to God, and in it, he arrogantly assumes the
role of God because He ". . . forgot how and when to be God."
He boasts in his letter:

I did what You did not, could not, would not do: I looked at that ugly
little black girl, and I loved her. I played You. And it was a very good
show! (143)

Soaphead uses Pecola to give some definitive meaning to his
own life and to substantiate his own identity; and like Cholly,
he further seals her fate by permanently separating her from
any meaningful potentialities within the community. Imprisoned now behind her illusion of blue eyes, Pecola escapes into
schizophrenia and silence.

Pecola's life has exhausted itself into the mythmetic act of
the male robbing the female of her identity. She, like Ovid's
Philomela, has had her tongue cut out by an act which has
inverted the natural order of her life. Her child is born too
soon and dies. "The damage done [is] total," Claudia recalls
(158). And thus like Philomela who turns into a nightingale,
Pecola, too, tries to transform herself and transcend the
mutilation of her life: ". . . she flailed her arms like a bird in
an eternal, grotesquely futile effort to fly" (158). But the
mythic rites of nature and life within her story have become
too cruelly inverted for her to do anything but ". . . [pick] and
[pluck] her way between the tire rims and the sunflowers,
between Coke bottles and milkweed, among all the waste and
beauty of the world—which is what she herself was" (159).

The community, too, must share the blame for Pecola's
diminishment. She has throughout been made a scapegoat by
a neighborhood of people who themselves live their own
unnatural lives under the gaze of the dominant culture.
Pecola's silent, sacrificial presence, then, holds a symbolic
function for them: Trapped as we-objects, they find comfort in
Pecola's dissolution; as Claudia recalls, "All of us—all who
knew her—felt so wholesome after we cleaned ourselves on
her" (159). Contrasting themselves with Pecola, they
embolden their own worth, deny the incongruity and
inauthenticity of their own lives, and thus, as Claudia says,
". . . the horror at the heart of [Pecola's] yearning [becomes]
exceeded only by the evil of fulfillment" (158). Pecola's
madness serves to perpetuate one community's own illusions.

In one way, Pecola, in her madness, has triumphed over her condition; the community, by contrast, remains in a static state of denial and dissonance.   However, Pecola's sacrificial position in the novel also has a more hopeful purpose. Claudia has survived to tell her and Pecola's story; she has testified to the unnaturalness of black life; and as a consequence, she recognizes in retrospect that she and the community have failed Pecola.   For Pecola, as Claudia says, ". . . it's much, much, much too late" (160).   But it is implicit in this sorrowful recognition that Claudia's story serves as a point of departure in her own search for an authenticating self.

Chapter IV

Sula:

The Contradictions of Self and Place

Unlike the multi-layered, segmented narrative of *The Bluest Eye*, Morrison's second novel, *Sula* (1973), employs a third-person narrative that unfolds in a seemingly chronological manner. It begins in the year 1919 and proceeds with chapters titled "1920," "1922," "1927," "1937," and so on to the year "1965." But each chapter does not cover an entire year. Instead, each represents a particular event around which revolves its past, present, and future significance. Thus the narrative unfolds like a firmly interwoven oral folktale wherein time merely provides the focus for the events themselves while the past, present, and future collapse into a kind of synchronic action.

At the same time, Morrison establishes a distinct tone beyond the mournfully graphic realism of *The Bluest Eye*. The setting in *Sula* is an isolated neighborhood called "The Bottom"; but it is a neighborhood of a recent historical past, and therefore "The Bottom" and its inhabitants assume, like the narrative itself, a mythological quality. They and their environment appear drawn from the rich tradition of black folktale and legend, which also serves another purpose: Unlike *The Bluest Eye*, the inhabitants of "The Bottom" are not often prey to the extreme seduction of a dominant culture. Instead they are presented as having a world of their own, and thus the delimiting of an external gaze and the valorization of black values and traditions further emphasize Morrison's singluar concern for black life.

An examination of both community and its characters is and will continue to be a familiar motif in all of Morrison's novels.

But in *Sula*, this motif is played out most conspicuously in the dialectical tension between community as monolithic status quo and individual as subversive figure. The novel contains a family of self-sustaining black female characters: the matriarch, Eva Peace, her daughter, Hannah, and her granddaughter, the novel's protagonist, Sula Peace, who combine to provide a subversive counterpoint and, in doing so, provide the oppositional energy to redefine both selfhood and black womanhood.

1.

In that place where they tore the nightshade and blackberry patches from their roots to make room for the Medallion City Golf Course, there was once a neighborhood. (2)

The novel begins with the end to "The Bottom" — a neighborhood once isolated from and eventually destroyed by white progress in Medallion City, Ohio. In the narrator's retrospective account, we are given an Eatonville-like description where you might have seen ". . . a dark woman in a flowered dress doing a bit of cakewalk, a bit of black bottom, a bit of 'messing around' to the lively notes of a mouth organ" (4). But this tranquil remembrance belies a contradictory undercurrent in the neighborhood because beyond the laughter of the people "messing around," there remains "the adult pain that rest[s] somewhere under [their] eyelids" (4).

We have entered another black world of contradiction and inverted truth, for as the story leaps from end to beginning, we learn that "The Bottom" is not situated in the fertile bottomland of the valley but in the cold, barren hills. The naming of the neighborhood itself has influenced and affixed a reality upon "The Bottom." A slavemaster had bequeathed "The Bottom" to his newly freed slave, who was hoodwinked into believing it was "'the bottom[land] of heaven'" (5). Thus its present inhabitants have come to think of it as "a joke, a nigger joke" (4). They can think of it in no other way because, for them, laughter is one way of dealing with their pain. People here endure, and do so because and at the behest of their environment, ". . . where planting [is] backbreaking, where the soil slid[es] down and wash[es] away the seeds, and where the wind linger[s] all through the winter" (5). This need to endure, to survive, then, compels the people of "The Bottom" to value consistency and control as yet another way of dealing with contradiction and privation. How they maintain this communal mind-set is the subject of the first chapter, "1919," and sets the stage for the novel's dialectical tension.

2.

Except for World War II, nothing ever interfered with the celebration of National Suicide Day. (7)

National Suicide Day encapsulates the central ordering principle around which the people of "The Bottom" conduct their lives. Begun by Shadrack, a shell-shocked WWI veteran, National Suicide Day is a simple ritual performed each January Third wherein Shadrack parades ". . . through the Bottom . . . with a cowbell and a hangman's rope calling the people together" (14). In a brief flashback, we learn of Shadrack's horrific war experience and his two-year stay in a hospital mental ward. Shadrack returns to Medallion mentally ravaged, "not daring to acknowledge the fact that he didn't even know who or what he was . . . with no past, no language, no tribe, no source. . ." (12). In the chaos of war, Shadrack senses his own nothingness; and he seeks refuge in National Suicide Day as a way of controlling his fear of death:

It had to do with making a place for fear as a way of controlling it. He knew the smell of death and was terrified of it, for he could not antici-pate it. It was not death or dying that frightened him, but the unexpectedness of both. In sorting it all out, he hit on the notion that if one day a year were devoted to it, everybody could get it out of the way and the rest of the year would be safe and free. (14)

At first the townspeople are frightened by Shadrack; he is an unconventional character; "his eyes [are] so wild, his hair so long and matted. . ." that he threatens the neighborhood's sense of normalcy. But as the narrator tells us, "Once the people understood the boundaries and nature of his madness, they could fit him, so to speak, into the scheme of things." The community is able and willing to accommodate his message ". . . into their thoughts, into their language, into their lives" (15) because the "boundaries and nature" of it are in keeping with their own social philosophy of consistency and control. Like Shadrack, the neighborhood wishes to control the "unexpectedness" of not only death, but of life, too. As we are later told, the neighborhood ". . . did not believe Nature was ever askew—only inconvenient" (90). To survive any inconvenience, which is indeed their ultimate aim, the people of "The Bottom" seek to identify and define any evil or aberration in order to lessen their vulnerabilities of being both human and black. With recognition comes a position of passive resistance and/or absorption of any aberration into the essential fabric of their lives:

> In spite of their fear, they reacted to an oppressive oddity, or what they called evil days, with an acceptance that bordered on welcome. Such evil must be avoided, they felt, and precautions must naturally be taken to protect themselves from it. But they let it run its course, fulfill itself, and never invented ways either to alter it, to annihilate it or or to prevent its happening again. So also were they with people. (90)

In keeping with this position of passive resistance and absorption, the people of "The Bottom" organize their lives around National Suicide Day so that weddings are never held on January Third, simple coincidences are attributed to it, and even ". . . Reverend Deal [takes] it up, saying the same folk who [have] sense enough to avoid Shadrack's call [are] the ones who [insist] on drinking themselves to death or womanizing themselves to death." Their integral response, which "easily, quietly. . . [becomes] a part of the fabric. . ." (16) of their lives, reproduces the long and weighty African-American tradition of call-and-response.

In its traditional form, call-and-response is the oral and/or vocal interplay between singer/storyteller and the audience/community. In the written word, this interplay of voices was reproduced first in the 19th century transcriptions of oral African-American folktales. Later this same structural interplay was improvised upon by such early 20th century writers as Jean Toomer in his novel *Cane* and in Zora Neale Hurston's *Their Eyes Were Watching God*. Contemporary black women writers, like their literary progenitors, have also appropriated call-and-response as a means to promulgate black culture and as a medium for potential transformation that, in Morrison's *Sula*, functions on two levels of signification.

Shadrack calls to the neighborhood and the people of "The Bottom" continue the dialogue by responding to Shadrack's call of death in socially variant ways. Moreover, this continuing dialogue prefigures the call-and-response that will occur throughout the novel and, in particular, the interplay that will occur between Sula Peace's "call" to the neighborhood and their subsequent "response." But of further significance, the text's call-and-response also engages the reader in its continuing dialogue of improvisation and image-making. Like the preacher and the congregation, we, as readers, are called by the story (". . . there once was a neighborhood."), guided by its interplay of voices and myriad events, and compelled to join in by our continued reading response. By its very nature and presence, then, call-and-response within *Sula* affirms the contextual nature and fluidity of language and, in doing so, provides a structurally ironic contrast to the neighborhood's own vision of order and continuity.

In each subsequent chapter of *Sula*, the neighborhood's response to Shadrack's call of death is replicated both in the public and private realms. Like National Suicide Day, the characters and events presented in each chapter revolve around an individual specter of death. But as we have already seen, this specter of death assumes an inverted quality in "The Bottom." Rather than creating a potentially liberating synthesis, Shadrack's call becomes another guidepost for survival and continuity. Thus, in its version of call-and-response, the neighborhood "fixes" rather than improvises upon the call in spite and because of the instability of Nature, Time, and most of all, the unexpectedness of Death.

In the next two chapters of the novel, the narrator recalls the events that surround and preoccupy two very different families—the Wrights and the Peaces. The story of these two families further specifies the "boundaries and nature" of "The

Bottom," particularly in how female and male roles are linked to the neighborhood's concept of survival. At the same time, we are introduced to the novel's central friendship between Nel Wright and Sula Peace. It is a friendship that will span some twenty years and will encompass, on a private level, the dialectical tension that surrounds the public lives of the entire neighborhood.

3.

To further establish this dialectical tension, the chapter, "1920," concerns itself with ten-year-old Nel Wright and her small, immediate family. Like Geraldine of *The Bluest Eye*, Nel's mother, Helene, epitomizes "lady-like," conventional womanhood; as the daughter of a Creole prostitute, she submerges her own funky past under the mantle of respectable domesticity and survives within her community by cultivating a puritanical middle-class reserve. She is a very respected, "impressive woman" to the townspeople,

> [whose] dark eyes arched in a perpetual query about other people's manners. A woman who won all social battles with presence and a conviction of the legitimacy of her authority. Since there was no Catholic church in Medallion then, she joined the most conservative black church. And held sway. It was Helene who never turned her head in church when latecomers arrived; Helene who established the practice of seasonal altar flowers. . . . (18)

The apparent irony in the narrator's description of Helene reinforces her rigidity. That Helene is respected indicates that she is correctly playing the role ascribed to all women by the community. Her concerns are trivial right down to her disappointment that "the people in the Bottom refused to say Helene. They called her Helen Wright and left it at that" (18). Helene Wright is, in short, proud to maintain the stereotyped image of the middle-class domesticated housewife and mother. These same attitudes of propriety and orderliness she attempts to inculcate into Nel in hopes of suppressing any funky urges that her dauther may have:

Under Helene's hand the girl became obedient and polite. Any enthu-
siasms that little Nel showed were calmed by the mother until she drove
her daughter's imagination underground. (18)

But even though Helene represses Nel's imagination, she
cannot entirely eliminate it, especially in the midst of their
journey back to New Orleans. They go to attend the funeral
of Helene's grandmother who had taken Helene away from
her mother's brothel and raised her ". . . under the dolesome
eyes of a multicolored Virgin Mary, counseling her to be
constantly on guard for any sign of her mother's wild blood"
(17). Helene's repressed upbringing and her learned repres-
sive reaction to her daughter's upbringing represents a cycle
of what Mary Helen Washington in her "Black-Eyed Susans"
calls ". . . psychic violence that alienates [black women] from
their roots and cuts them off from real contact with their own
people and also from a part of themselves" (213).

In Helene's internalized position of self-alienation, returning to her "own people" and to "a part of herself" now
repressed bring out in her "all the old vulnerabilities, all the
old fears of being somehow flawed. . ." (20). Outside of her
"impressive" position in the Bottom, Helene must negotiate in
a world for which she has no control, and therefore her codes
of conduct will prove both futile and meaningless. All of
which is not lost on Nel who sees her mother unnecessarily
grovel before a white railroad ticketmaster, who, because of
their color, urinates with her in open fields at station stops;
and who watches her mother rejoice when she returns to the
safety of Mediallion. These instances expose the ironic unnaturalness of Helene's "tall, proud" life (22). She cannot survive
with any sense of dignity outside of the Bottom, but to retain
her dignity she must divorce herself from the world, from her
roots, and instead introject white middle-class stereotypes. For
her, the double jeopardy of being both woman and black is
"resolved" by remaining behind a physical and emotional veil.
And in a larger sense, Helene merely reflects an entire
community which itself survives and retains its collective
dignity through separation and introjection.

For Nel, on the other hand, the trip awakens in her new possibilities for awareness and growth.   Her idealism is kindled by her exposure to Southern segregation, but more importantly, she senses the distortion and alienation of her mother's life.   She makes a promise to herself that she will never be "turn[ed] . . . into jelly" by the look of the white man because, as the narrator says, ". . . if [Helen] were really custard, then there was a chance that Nel was too" (22).   Upon her return from New Orleans, Nel thinks about the trip, about "the gardenia smell" and "canary-yellow dress" (25) of her grandmother's.   She thinks about the obvious differences between Creole and Medallion societies, and in the process of thought, Nel objectifies her own sense of enforced alienation and whispers: "'I'm me. I'm not their daughter. I'm not Nel. I'm me. Me'" (28).   Nel's experiences prompt her to look outside of herself, outside of her mother's system of self-denial.

Nel has been called by a new and vibrant world, and her response triggers a period of re-seeing her life and environment.   Through her retrospection, she begins to envision new potentialities in her life: "For days afterward she imagined other trips she would take. . ." (29).   More significantly, it is one of many instances in which Nel will re-see an event; she becomes a kind of surrogate reader who experiences and (re)examines events.   She and, in turn, the reader, continually need to rethink and change their perceptions. As a narrative technique, this flexibility of perspective reinforces the fluidity and improvisational nature of call and response, and throughout the novel continually serves to undercut the ordered stance of the neighborhood. Nel, for her part, seeks a radical change through her retrospection, and therefore, as the narrator tells us, "The trip, perhaps, or her new found me-ness, [gives] her the strength to cultivate a friend in spite of her mother" (29). That friend is Sula Peace.

4.

Sula Peace lived in a house of many rooms that had been built over a period of five years to the specifications of its owner, who kept on adding things: more stairways—there were three sets to the second floor—more rooms, doors and stoops. There were rooms that had three doors, others that opened out on the porch only and were inaccessible from any other part of the house; others that you could get to only by going through somebody's bedroom. (30)

The antithesis to the order and continuity of Helene Wright and to the neighborhood in general could not be more clearly signified than in the structural description of the Peace home. In contrast to the self-reflexive "oppressive neatness" (29) of the Wright home, the Peace house reflects the apparent disorderliness and complexity of the women who live there—a family so apparently different from Helene and the neighborhood that they exasperate "the 'good' women" (44) in the town by their seeming lack of decorum and order.

That the Peace house has been built under "the specifications of its owner," however, indicates that the house's unpeacefulness and chaos have a deliberate design. There is a restlessly manipulative energy embodied in the "owner(s)" of this house. One owner is Eva Peace who sits ". . . in a wagon on the third floor directing the lives. . ." (30) of her family and of anyone else who happens by. The other owner is the storyteller/narrator who, in Chapter "1921," begins to both enlarge and dissolve the story's dialectical tension.

Eva's home is plainly Bedlam, inhabited not only by three generations of Peace women: Eva, Hannah, and Sula; but also by Eva's son, Plum; three orphaned children, all named Dewey; and by Tar Baby, an alcoholic bachelor. Eva encourages a communal atmosphere to develop around her and welcomes any and all outsiders, ". . . cousins who [are] passing through, stray folks, and the many, many newly married couples. . ." (37). Her affinity to a social collectivity springs from a past life of abandonment and deprivation; as the narrator tells it, Eva had been deserted by her husband, Boy-Boy, "after five years of a sad and disgruntled marriage. . ." (32). With three children to feed and care for, she valiantly struggles to survive while living a hand-to-mouth existence. Faced with this futile future, she leaves her children with neighbors and sets out like the traditional black male runner. Eighteen months later, Eva returns to Medallion with ten-thousand dollars and without a leg; she thereafter "reclaims her children" and starts "building a house on Carpenter's Road. . ."

(34-35). Neighborhood gossip contends that Eva had allowed a train to sever her leg in order to collect the insurance money, but "whatever the fate of her lost leg. . ." (31), the effect of Eva's past life positions her in the text as the embodiment of a black feminist self-determinism that defied the odds against abandoned black women in 1921.

Eva's character, however, is infinitely more complex than that of the stereotypically suffering and self-sacrificing black woman. In contrast to the kind, religious, asexual white-folk's mammy, Eva displays a multiplicity and intensity of emotions which align her more closely with the traditional mammy of oral folk tales. Practical and commonsensical, she is also arrogant, domineering, and mean-spirited. By her collectivized presence she consciously subverts the mind-set of the neighborhood, while all the time remaining withdrawn in her third-story bedroom. Furthermore, her entire self-sustaining perspective is fueled by her hatred for Boy-Boy: "Knowing that she would hate him long and well filled her with pleasant anticipation . . . it was hating him that kept her alive and happy" (36-7).

In some ways, then, Eva presents a clear antithesis to the Bottom's ordering principle. Her many-sided characteristics, her disrupted and mutilated life, and the spontaneity of her household all typify a kind of angularity in her life, what Zora Neale Hurston in her *The Sanctified Church* defines as the African-American determination "to avoid the straight line" (54). Her life, as recounted in the text, reflects this angularity, where present and past intersect, where the past informs and transforms her present. And thus as an antithesis to the middle-class mimicry of the Bottom, Eva lives within an African-American communality that is further described by Hurston as being lived within ". . . the rhythm of segments. Each unity has rhythm of its own, but when the whole is assembled it is lacking in symmetry" (55). This lack of symmetry is something Helene could never tolerate, could never assimilate into her class-conscious society.

But there remains a necessary contradcition in Eva's position; as Leon S. Roudiez comments in his "Introduction" to Julia Kristeva's *Desire in Language*,

... there is contradiction inherent in all things, which results in a cleavage, a struggle between the two elements of the contradiction, elimination of the weaker element, and then, within the victorious one, there is contradiction, etc. (14)

Helene Wright and the neighborhood are "frightened," fearful, vulnerable, scornful; the inhabitants of the Carpenter's Road house are fanciful, "funky," "sweet," "spontaneous." The narrator's word choice alone can determine whom the reader should sympathize with and which "element" within the story's dialectic should therefore assume a "victorious" position. An inevitable contradiction does appear, however, in Eva's victorious position: It is the absence of a loving, sensitive center in her character that is particularly significant because it leaves a dangerous void of indifference and obliviousness in the lives of her children and in their children.

In echoing a community opinion, the narrator says that "with the exception of Boy-Boy, those Peace women loved all men. It was manlove that Eva bequeathed to her daughters" (41). And indeed, Eva's daughter, Hannah, "exasperate[s]" the "good women" of the Bottom because she ". . . simply refuse[s] to live without the attentions of a man." She is a consummate lover who "ripple[s] with sex" (44, 42) and who teaches her own daughter, Sula, by example, that ". . . sex [is] pleasant and frequent, but otherwise unremarkable" (44). Eva, for her part, has ". . . a regular flock of gentlemen callers, and although she [does] not participate in the act of love, there [is] a good deal of teasing and pecking and laughter" (41). In these various depictions of Eva and Hannah, one could argue that their lives exemplify the womanist stance of simplicity, intimacy, and communal candor. Both women are self-sustaining in their respective roles and do not appear to succumb to the neighborhood's ordering principle; they ". . . simply [love] maleness for its own sake" (41).

While there is nothing inherently problematic in Eva's and Hannah's self-sustaining, oppositional positions in the neighborhood—indeed they present a lively alternative to its stasis—their apparently womanist positions should not be perceived as necessarily different from the neighborhood's ordering principle. Hannah is "fastidious about whom she [sleeps] with, [but] she [will] fuck practically anything" (43); and she does so with no sense of commitment or passion. She is not, however, a conventional seductress; she makes no demands on the men she knows and she is genuinely honest about her affairs. As the narrator puts it, "she [can] break up a marriage before it [has] even become one—she [can] make love to the new groom and wash his wife's dishes all in an afternoon." After the death of her husband, Hannah has no desire to remarry, she simply wants to have "some touching every day" (44). But Hannah's independence obscures her acute inability to communicate love; it is an inability learned from Eva, and in spite of Hannah's overt womanism, her inability to love deeply troubles her.

In her interview with Robert Stepto, Morrison says of Hannah that "she [has] no concept of love and possession. She like[s] to be laid, she like[s] to be touched but she [doesn't] want any confusion of relationships and so on." Morrison reserves much harsher criticism for Eva who, as she says,

> . . . kills her son, plays god, names people and, you know, puts her hand on a child. You know, she's god-like, she manipulates—all in the best interest. And she is very, very possessive about other people, that is, as a king is. (487)

"'Mamma, did you ever love us?'" Hannah asks of Eva, to which Eva responds, "'No. I don't reckon I did. Not the way you thinkin'" (67). Hannah's question comes two years after Eva had burned to death her only son, Plum. In chapter "1921," we had been given only scant details of his death. Now a further history and retrospection compels us to again re-see an event. Plum had been a war veteran who, upon his return, had become a drug addict and, in his drug-induced state, had reverted to infancy. At the same time that Hannah asks her about love, she also wonders why Eva had killed Plum, and Eva tells her that Plum had tried "'. . . to get back up in my womb'" (72). She had no sympathy for his weakness and thought only that Plum should "'. . . go on and live and be a man'": "'I had to keep him out so I just thought of a way he could die like a man not all scrunched up inside my womb, but like a man'" (72).

Eva sets her son's bed on fire and, in doing so, underscores her own lack of a loving, sensitive center. It is a center that long ago was diffused in desperation by her need to assume a position of pragmatic matriarch, possessive and domineering. And thus when Hannah continues to wonder why Eva didn't love her children, she counters by saying,

> "No time. They wasn't no time. Not none. Soon as I got one day done here come a night. With you all coughin' and me watchin' so TB wouldn't take you off and if you was sleepin' quiet I thought, O Lord, they dead and put my hand over your mouth to feel if the breath was comin' what you talkin' 'bout did I love you girl I stayed alive for you can't you get that through your thick head or what is that between your ears, heifer?" (69)

Like Helene, Eva, too, has been driven to a state of unnaturalness; there is "no time" for anything but to "stay alive," to survive; and while each character does so in her own radically different way, each necessarily sacrifices love for some sense of order and continuity within their respective households. And thus, both Helene and Eva are inextricably linked to the ordering principle of the Bottom, and in spite of Eva's outlandish and taboo behavior, neither character genuinely threatens the essential fabric of the neighborhood; they accept similar conventionalized values; Helene assumes a rigid, middle-class mind-set; Eva presumes an unyielding despotism. As we shall later see, their subjective acceptance inhibits them from challenging the very limitations of these roles. Interspaced within this dissolving tension and unstable alliance is yet another: the friendship of Sula and Nel.

Following Hannah's questioning of her mother, she, too, is tragically burned to death in a yard-fire that is perhaps Nature's and Hannah's revenge against Eva's taboo murder of her son. Several omens foreshadow the event, most strategically, a powerfully hot summer wind. These seemingly insignificant omens all point to the neighborhood's futility in their attempts at controlling Nature and Death. However, more important than the event itself is Sula's reaction to watching her mother burn to death. As a testament of her unusual character, we learn that Eva ". . . [remains] convinced that Sula [has] watched Hannah burn not because she [is] paralyzed, but because she [is] interested" (78).

5.

> Because [Nel and Sula] had discovered years before that they were neither white nor male, and that all freedom and triumph was forbidden to them, they had set about creating something else to be. Their meeting was fortunate, for it let them use each other to grow on. Daughters of distant mothers and incomprehensible fathers (Sula's because he was dead; Nel's because he wasn't), they found in each other's eyes the intimacy they were looking for. (52)

Two convergent critical analyses posit that the attraction between Sula and Nel centers upon either a unification of the divided self or upon their latent, erotic desire for each other. Both analyses are based upon the preceding passage. For instance, Naana Banyiwa-Horne argues that Sula and Nel ". . . experience total harmony when they are together" and that therefore ". . . neither . . . feels the need to assert her separate identity" (29). The narrator reinforces this unification by stating that ". . . it was in dreams that the two girls had first met." Each girl has ". . . Technicolor visions that always [include] a presence, a someone, who quite like the dream, [share] the delight of the dream" (51). Banyiwa-Horne contends that "the groping of two girls for each other in their dreams echoes the groping of the unconscious self to embrace its conscious part. . ." (29). The convergence of their divided selves, therefore, creates in Sula and Nel a singular identity that becomes, as Banyiwa-Horne continues, "a balanced, healthy personality" (29). The healthy Sula-Nel has what each lacks alone: Nel looks to break free from her mother's smothering constancy and sees in Sula the potential for creativity and imagination; Sula, whose mother ". . . never scolded or gave directions" (29), looks to Nel as a guidepost to her own wayward imagination. Together, they affirm their mutual strengths and recreate themselves as one; and thus, as the narrator states, "in the safe harbor of each other's company they [can] afford to abandon the ways of other people and concentrate on their own perceptions of things" (55).

The same dream passage provides evidence for Barbara Smith's interpretation of the Sula/Nel attraction. Smith argues that the passage ". . . shows their relationship, from the very beginning, is suffused with an erotic romanticism. The dreams in which they are initially drawn to each other are actually complementary aspects of the same sensuous fairytale" (166). Nel imagines herself lying in bed and "waiting for some fiery prince" who "never quite" arrives; Sula dreams that she gallops "on a gray and white horse . . . in full view of a some-one" who shares her dream (*Sula* 51-52). Both Banyiwa-Horne's and Smith's critiques converge at this moment of attraction, but Smith goes further by implying that since Sula and Nel are joined together in their "erotic" dreams and since "they are neither white nor male," their relationship has a lesbian quality to it. Smith stops short of stating directly that the girls' relationship is "inherently lesbian" as she claims that Morrison refutes any such interpretation. Her aim, she says, in locating the lesbian potentiality in the novel is simply ". . . to point out how a Black feminist critical perspective at least allows consideration of this level of the novel's meaning" (170). However, she does engage in a reader's somewhat disturbing but ordinary fancy to rewrite the text; she comments that, "the work might be clearer still if Morrison had approached her subject with the consciousness that a lesbian relationship was at least a possibility for her characters. . ." (170).

Smith's wishful reading recalls a past African-American criticism that would also yearn for clarity and logic in the furtherance of a specific ideology. But more importantly, that *Sula* should have been an overtly lesbian text distorts what is the central interpretative attraction between Sula and Nel. Clearly, as Banyiwa-Horne maintains, the novel reveals a one-ness in the girls' mutuality; separately they function poorly. And certainly Nel and Sula, at certain moments in the text, sustain a loving friendship which has sensual qualities. But their attraction is more specifically located in their reactionary desire for Nel's "me-ness" or, as Sula says, for ". . . the closest thing to both an other and a self . . . Nel was the first person who had been real to her, whose name she knew. . ." (119-20).

Apart, both Sula and Nel remain isolated in their non-identities; both girls know only a conformity to patriarchal convention and values which their households approve of and accept. Unified, they represent an antithesis to patriarchal conventions that is embodied in the fluidity and improvisational nature of their relationship.

In her interview with Robert Stepto, Morrison explains that in *Sula* she wanted to elaborate on ". . . a very old, worn-out idea, which was to do something with good and evil, but putting it in different terms" (475). By the nature of their upbringing and thus as they are perceived by the neighborhood, Nel and Sula do seem to represent the potential for "good" and "evil"; or, in other words, in relation to community value constructs, Nel epitomizes good, conventional values and Sula aspires to rebellion. But Morrison puts good and evil "in different terms" by first detailing Nel's potential for conventional womanhood and then melding her seeming strength and consistency (53) with Sula who, by narrative design, has heretofore been given little narrative attention.

Each brief glimpse of Sula, along with Nel's attraction to her, creates both contradiction and anticipation: Who is this girl who, as Eva believes, watches with interest as her mother burns to death; who, as the narrator tells us, can "hardly be counted on to sustain any emotion for more than three minutes" (53); who overhears her mother say that she "loves" her, but who adds, "'I just don't like her'" (57); and who is genuinely liked by Helene because she seems "to have none of the mother's slackness" (29)? Like the neighborhood itself, the reader is allowed to see Nel as a "good" girl who only dreams; she is thus a paradigm of passive patriarchal expectations. In contrast, Sula's position, like her household, fluctuates and therefore cannot be clearly fixed by both reader and community alike.

In chapter "1922," two scenes underscore Sula's indeterminacy and serve to determine the direction of her remaining life. Both Nel and Sula are intent upon adventuresomeness" (55). But it is Sula who instigates such adventure. For example, Sula convinces Nel to take the "shortest way" home in anticipation of meeting "four white boys" who have been "harrassing black schoolchildren," including Nel (54, 53). In their encounter, Sula pulls a knife, which makes "the boys stop short," and proceeds to "slash off only the tip of her finger" (54). In her effort to protect Nel, Sula assumes the role of active victim while appearing recklessly indifferent. Nel, in her passivity, can only look at Sula's face "which seem[s] miles and miles away" (55).

The second and more unsettling scene involves the death of a young child. A good part of chapter "1922" details the two twelve-year-old girls' budding interest in the neighborhood's "beautiful black boys" (56). But like many of the novel's chapters, what begins as self-discovery ends in frustration and constriction of expectations, which are symbolized through death or betrayal. Toward the close of the chapter, the girls meet Chicken Little by the river bank and again Sula plays an active and purposeful role by helping the elated, small boy to climb a tree. After they descend from the tree, Sula continues her playfulness by picking up Chicken by his hands and swinging him around and around until she accidentally loses her grip and the boy sails into the river. Both girls watch helplessly as Chicken Little drowns. Nel believes that "'Somebody saw'," and since Shadrack's isolated cabin is the only one near, Sula, the activist, runs to ask him.

With Shadrack absent, Sula enters his home and is surprised by its "neatness and order." Her childhood fear of "the terrible Shad" is dispelled and when she turns to see him in the doorway, he punctuates the frustration of expectations that surround the text by simply saying, "'Always'" (61-62). His intention as he believes many years later is "to convince her, assure her of permanency" (157). Shadrack has not seen the accident, and thus his vision of controlling death remains intact. He has, however, had a visitor to his lonely home which will have a great influence upon his later life and upon the entire neighborhood. But at the moment of their encounter, Sula misreads Shadrack's "always," believing it to be linked to what she begins to see as the constant untrustworthiness of human experience.

Later in the novel, Sula, as an adult, re-sees her active childhood and provides an explanation for her actions. She has carried with her the recognition that "the one time she tried to protect Nel . . . earned not Nel's gratitude but her disgust" (141). This incident and her remembrance, coupled with the death of Chicken Little and the recognition of her mother's dislike for her, have taught her that ". . . there was no self to count on either" (119). But Sula's explanation is, of course, withheld from the reader, from Nel, and from the neighborhood so that for much of the novel, we feel torn and nonplussed about Sula; we waver in our perceptions of her, which is symbolically reinforced by the birthmark on her face. At various times throughout the novel, it is made analogous to a tadpole by Shadrack, a copperhead snake by Nel's husband, Jude, a stemmed rose by Nel, and a frightening "black thing" by Nel's children. Like her birthmark, Sula becomes the center of ambivalence in the novel that both attracts and repels us perhaps because, as Banyiwa-Horne contends, "Sula is . . . an exploration of that dimension of the feminine psyche or self which is often hidden from view because it is scary and too problematic to deal with." Banyiwa-Horne goes on to say that ". . . this scary self exists in all women and, for that matter, in all human beings" (28), and it specifically seeks to break free from social and cultural convention. Having "no self to count on," Sula seeks an alternative self that is, as the narrator says,

> . . . completely free of ambition, with no affection for money, property or things, no greed, no desire to command attention or compliments—no ego. For that reason she [feels] no compulsion to verify herself—be consistent with herself. (119)

Sula's reactionary realizations create a fissure between Sula and Nel which points to the inherent contradiction in their call and response synthesis. While Sula reacts to Chicken Little's unanticipated death with her own kind of free-fall away from social and emotional expectations, Nel retreats to the safety of the familiar fixed principles of the Bottom. The divergent paths of the two women offer two perspectives on communal reality. Nel responds to Chicken's death much as the community might do with what she later realizes as a "calm, controlled behavior" (170). As a product of her upbringing, she, like her mother, assumes the controlling response attributable to National Suicide Day as she demystifies inconstancy by re-initiating her white, middle-class values. Four years later she chooses to marry a local boy, Jude, and she sublimates her "me-ness" for the certitude of marriage because, as she thinks, ". . . greater than her friendship [with Sula is] this new feeling of being needed by someone who saw her singly" (84).

Like Helene, Nel becomes exactly what the community wishes her to be. It is an all-too-familiar process of commodification wherein Nel is used for the gratification and reinforcement of patriarchal order. Unable to find employment and thus respectability, Jude imagines that being married to Nel can give him "some posture of adulthood" (82); that a wife can somehow fill the void of economic and emotional incompleteness in his life:

> Whatever his fortune, whatever the cut of his garment, there would always be the hem—the tuck and fold that hid his raveling edges; a someone sweet, industrious and loyal to shore him up. (83)

And Nel, for her part, willingly wishes to be an objectified nonentity; she finds solace in the stereotype of the loving, dutiful wife precisely because she, too, seeks protection from Nature, Time, and the unexpectedness of Death. (127). In short, Jude and Nel are equally products of a community which looks to whatever kind of controlling mechanism that may protect them from the impingements of the world.

In Sula, however, Morrison creates a character who wishes to break free from this social cycle of denial and certitude. She wishes to create her own reality which thrives upon the fluidity and free-play of call and response and does not seek Bottom-like constructs as an affrontery to contradiction and chaos. While Nel attempts to find her self and place in her childhood dream for "some fiery prince," Sula leaves the Bottom seeking her own dream "of herself galloping on a horse at top speed." She becomes the archetypal "running man" of American literature who seeks a physical as well as emotional freedom from the order and control of society. Because her travels will be unstructured and nondirectional, they will reinforce her noncommittal position; "hers," as the narrator later comments, "[is] an experimental life" (118). Thus ends Part One of *Sula*; on the very day of Nel's wedding, Sula departs from the Bottom, and thereafter Nel's and Sula's relationship will remain forever changed. Yet in the death of their once thriving friendship will commence another dialectical process between Sula and the community.

6.

> Accompanied by a plague of robins, Sula came back to Medallion. The little yam-breasted shuddering birds were everywhere, exciting very small children away from their usual welcome into a vicious stoning. Nobody knew why or from where they had come. What they did know was that you couldn't go anywhere without stepping in their pearly shit, and it was hard to hang up clothes, pull weeds or just sit on the front porch when robins were flying and dying all around you. (89)

Part Two begins with Sula's ominous return to the Bottom. We know nothing of her wanderings, and only much later are we given a definitive perspective upon why she returns. On her travels "she had been looking all along for a friend" (121), or more specifically, as she later realizes, Sula had been looking for her own sense of "me-ness" which, with Nel, she had had all along: "Nel was the only person who had wanted nothing from her. . ." (119). Nel had allowed her simply to be and become rather than prompt her to conform to the Bottom's ordering principles. But as the signs of nature portend, Sula's return will only create chaos and resistance within the community because, after ten years, Nel has grown accustomed to her guarded life and, more importantly, because the whole of the Bottom's inhabitants cannot and will not respond to Sula's improvisational call.

Eva sets the tone for the community's attitude toward the prodigal Sula: "'When you gone to get married? You need to have some babies, it'll settle you.'" To which Sula replies, "'I don't want to make somebody else. I want to make myself'" (92). And in her first act of rebellion against the community's order, the arrogant and belligerent Sula ironically dethrones Eva from her position of arrogance and presumption and forceably has her removed to a nursing home. Sula's act firmly announces to the community her contempt for Eva's pronouncements; as the community will come to learn, "Sula [is] distinctly different. Eva's arrogance and Hannah's self-indulgence merge in her and . . . she live[s] out her days exploring her own thoughts and emotions. . ." (118).

For Nel, Sula's return rekindles long-cherished memories of her childhood friendship. As Nel always knew, Sula's presence in her life offers Nel "a constant sharing of perceptions':

> Talking to Sula had always been a conversation with herself. Was there anyone else before whom she could never be foolish? In whose view inadequacy was mere idiosyncrasy, a character trait rather than a deficiency? Anyone who left behind that aura of fun and complicity? Sula never completed; she simply helped others define themselves. (95)

Nel re-sees in Sula her other self—a self which she has long buried in respectability: "She felt new, soft and new. It had been the longest time since she had had a rib-scraping laugh" (98). But Nel's sense of newness and redefinition is illusionary and short-lived; she and Sula have clearly taken two different roads in life. And nothing more definitely shatters this illusion as when Nel finds Sula making love with Jude.

It is clearly an act of betrayal by Jude and especially by Sula whose friendship had meant so much to Nel. Sula's taboo act demonstrates that her non-committal stance will challenge the very foundations of marriage or any other convention. But the focus during and after this encounter is not on Jude's or Sula's motivations, instead the narrator focuses upon Nel's perceptions and reactions to this moment of sexuality. In many ways, the remainder of the novel will be Nel's story wherein she must see and re-see Sula's inexplicably shocking behavior in order for her to come to terms with her own behavior and sets of values. In first seeing the moment, Nel, in spite of her shock, is concerned only with propriety and appearances. Only Jude appears naked to Nel while Sula does not, and as the moment of sexuality lingers, Nel's biggest concern after the two lovers dress is that Jude's fly remains open:

> . . . me wanting her to leave so I could tell you privately that you had forgotten to button your fly because I didn't want to say it in front of her, Jude. And even when you began to talk, I couldn't hear because I was worried about you not knowing that your fly was open. . . . (106)

For Nel, to see the inconstant is to repress the inconstant. It is Jude, the man for whom she has loved and lived who must be protected, covered, and made respectable once again just as Nel herself will again be respectable. She regains her respectability but at the price of losing her husband and ending her friendship with Sula. As she sits in her bathroom, "small enough to contain her grief" (107), she rationalizes that "Sula was wrong. Hell ain't things lasting forever. Hell is change." Crouched in the bathroom, Nel waits "for the oldest cry. . . , a deeply personal cry for one's own pain," but "her very own howl" does not come (108). Left instead is "something just to the right of her, in the air, just out of view. She [cannot] see it, but she [knows] exactly what it look[s] like. A gray ball hovering just there" (108-9).

Her pain and fear of loss and change become in her mind a dirty ball of fur and string which she of course avoids seeing, "for if she saw it, who could tell but what she might actually touch it, or want to, and then what would happen if she actually reached out her hand and touched it" (110). If Nel touches the dirty ball she confronts her constructed self and place within the community and shatters her illusion that her life, as well as the lives of the entire community, exist without loss, without change, without control. Unlike Sula, whose realizations that inconstancy and contradiction offer the potential for exploration, Nel now believes that since "her thighs [are] truly empty" and since her transcendent friendship is gone, there is nothing left but to live fully in fear of experience, of both pain and pleasure. Even Sula perceives Nel as "now . . . one of them":

> One of the spiders, who dangled in the dark dry places suspended by their own spittle, more terrified of the free fall than the snake's breath below. Their eyes so intent on the wayward stranger who trips into their net, they were blind to the cobalt on their backs. . . . (120)

From Sula's perspective, she is that wayward stranger who, through her seemingly insensate behavior, has challenged the attitudes and values which Nel and the community have held dear but which, in the end, leave them devoid of their own "me-ness." Unlike them, Sula seeks "a full surrender to the downward flight" in order for her "to stay alive" (120). Like Hannah, Sula sleeps with the town's husbands, but unlike her mother who seemed to "[compliment] the women, in a way, by wanting their husbands," Sula "[tries] them out and discard[s] them without any excuse the men [can] swallow" (115). Sula is not interested in love, sexual gratification, or even simple human contact, she wishes instead, as she does with all of her exploratory gestures, to visibly demonstrate the community's certitude and conformity and, as a result, create her own form.

But even though her own form is designed to allow her to do more than merely survive, as do the townspeople, her attempts at "invention" are met not merely with disapproval, but with, as the narrator says, "all minds . . . closed to her" (120). Sula's rebellious acts predictably place her in a pariah position; all her attempts at an experientially guiltless and egoless life ironically lead her not to identity or community, but to an ultimate sense of solitude and isolation. And thus she learns this truth: an experimental life, especially for a woman, leads only to ostracism, loneliness, and ultimately to a descent "down howling, howling in a stinging awareness of the ending of things" (123).

But Morrison knows that the truth of the two women's lives lies somewhere between the actuality of Nel's loss and pain and Sula's extremist behavior and her unrelenting view that the town's women have "folded themselves into starched coffins" (122). Sula herself discovers the need for consistency and control as the author juxtaposes Sula's extremism with her relationship to Ajax, a man whom she had known since childhood and who, after hearing "all the stories about Sula," has begun calling on her because "her elusiveness and indifference to established habits of behavior remind him of this mother. . ." (127). In all of Morrison's novels, the love relationship that develops between Sula and Ajax is perhaps her most perfectly conceived. By its very nature, their relationship evokes Hurston's classic relationship between Janie and Teacake in *Their Eyes Were Watching God*.

Like Janie, Sula is pleased because Ajax treats her as an equal: "They had genuine conversations. He did not speak down to her or at her. . ." (127-8). And he thinks of her as a self-sustaining individual, refusing "to baby or protect her," believing "that she [is] both tough and wise. . ." (128). They also complement one another in their desire for adventure and free-flight. Next to Sula, Ajax's greatest love is airplanes; he loves to watch them fly and often dreams of himself in flight: ". . . he thought of airplanes, and pilots, and the deep sky that held them both" (126). Flying for Ajax symbolizes his desire not only to resist limitation, but to escape consistency and control; thus, in each other, the two lovers find another version of themselves. But in having discovered this primary bond, Sula also begins "to discover what possession [is]" (131). And although it is an "alien" feeling for Sula, she cultivates the sensation through homemaking activities, and tells Ajax to lean on her. This specter of dependence and possession, which weighs so heavily in other community relationships, is enough to frighten Ajax away and make him return to his vision of planes and flight.

In Ajax's absence, Sula, like Nel, experiences the similar pain of loss and change. She, too, cannot now deny her membership to the community as she comes to realize that in her possessiveness, she had never known Ajax's full name. She only sought to possess him in order to create, in her own way, a respectable haven similar to Nel's. Adding this loss to Sula's isolation heightens her sense that she has "sung all the songs" (137) in her life, and therefore there is nothing left to do but die. In her state of loss, isolation, and finally death, Sula depolarizes the distance between herself and the community, and especially between herself and Nel. Loss and change, in the face of community constructs of consistency and control, reach deeply into the psyches of Sula and Nel and leave them both lingering in a kind of living death. All doors to a meaningful self and place in the community are closed to them; Sula is struck down for attempting both exploration and conformity; Nel, for her self-diminishing wish for respectability and survival. And only Sula draws the distinction between both women when she speaks to Nel on her deathbed:

"You think I don't know what your life is like just because I ain't living it. I know what every colored woman in this country is doing."
"What's that?"
"Dying. Just like me. But the difference is they dying like a stump. Me, I'm going down like one of those redwoods. I sure did live in this world." (143)

But in the end, Sula has not found fulfillment or a self-sustaining focus in her life. "'Girl, I got my mind'" (143), Sula tells Nel, but left without a context, to turn inward upon the self proves just as futile as any reliance upon experience, upon Ajax, or upon a conformist society. Like the repressed artistry of Pauline in *The Bluest Eye*, Sula has "had no center, no speck around which to grow" (119). Her destructive life has been, as the narrator says, the consequences of "an idle imagination": "And like any artist with no art form, she became dangerous" (121).

7.

"You can't do it all. You a woman and a colored woman at that. You can't act like a man. You can't be walking around all independent-like, doing what you like, taking what you want, leaving what you don't." (142)

Sula has been defeated by Nel's community truism, and therein lies the tragedy of her story; she does not, like Janie in *Their Eyes Were Watching God*, return triumphant to meet her accusers. She cannot sustain an imaginative self and place within her community. (131). And at first, the Bottom's inhabitants are pleased to learn of her death: "the death of Sula Peace was the best news folks up in the Bottom had had since the promise of work at the tunnel" (150).

But soon, in the absence of the supposed evil of Sula, the community is left devoid of a perceptable dialectic. What is good without the presence of evil? How may one measure one's righteousness without the presence of a pariah, an evil? In a very short time, the Bottom without its pariah begins to collapse upon itself. Mothers who guarded their children, and wives who protected their husbands now take to arguing among themselves, and thereby dissolve their unity which the perceived opposition of Sula brought to them: "A falling away, a dislocation was taking place. Hard on the heels of the general relief Sula's death brought a restless irritability took hold. . ." (153). In death as well as in life, Sula remains a force for change in the community which, in Morrison's complex world, presents both negative and positive ramifications.

The community collapses and does so at the instigation of the very person who has inspired all conceptualized affrontry to contradiction and inconsistency. When Sula dies, Shadrack realizes that death cannot be forestalled; there is no "always" for anyone: "His visitor was dead and would come no more" (158). He therefore leads the entire community on National Suicide Day not now to scare death away, but to embrace it. The community, on the other hand, hopes to rekindle a sense of unification so resolutely lost in the absence of Sula's evil presence. Therefore, they follow Shadrack blindly but cheerfully to a construction tunnel which, as blacks, they have been forbidden to build. What they seek, as the narrator says, is a ". . . respite from anxiety, from dignity, from the weight of that very adult pain that [has] undergirded them" (160). They try to destroy the tunnel, but in their one defiant act to rid themselves and their town from being "a nigger joke," they cause the tunnel to collapse, and they bury themselves in the carnage as Shadrack simply watches, "having forgotten his song and his rope. . . ." (162).

In a singular moment of impulse, the majority of the townspeople are killed; they can neither survive the intrusion of the dominant culture nor the inevitability of death. Thus the failure of their survivalist mechanisms point to the apparent realization that, as Barbara Christian comments, ". . . human beings have to demand more from life than mere survival, or they may not survive at all. To really live life, there must be some imagination, some exploration, so there can be some creative action" (174). This may be the primary idea in Morrison's novel, but it is clear throughout that she carefully avoids valorizing the mere presence of imagination and exploration as a means to creative action. Instead, Morrison reveals the inherent limitations of both the independent "new" and the survivalist "old": free-flight without purpose and certitude without fluidity are equally unwieldy and, in the end, they serve to undermine human creativity.

Morrison offers no clear resolution to this conflict. Ironically, in the final chapter, 24 years after the death of Sula and the dissolution of the Bottom, neither the need for survival nor the need for independence impacts the remaining black population in Medallion. If there had been a semblance of cohesiveness within the Bottom, regardless of how tenuous that cohesiveness may have been, Nel now perceives that the Bottom's descendants, "for all their new look, [seem] awfully anxious to . . . abandon the hills to whoever [is] interested" (166). Blacks, who have benefitted from the civil rights movement, now work in main street stores and teach in the schools, but instead of seeking a "real place," a place that might be called a community, Nel sees that "now there [aren't] any places left, just separate houses with separate televisions and separate telephones and less and less dropping by" (166). This desire for separateness leaves Medallion's blacks, like their white counterparts, corrupted by a society's obsession with personal gain, and attracted to a "me-ness" far removed from Nel's childhood conception.

In this atmosphere of impasse, ambivalence, and indistinction, Nel weaves her way through the fractured town on her way to its nursing home. She wishes to visit Eva Peace, one of the few acquaintances she has left in the town. Her visit is a moment of epiphany as Eva accuses Nel of killing Chicken Little:

> "I didn't throw no little boy in the river. That was Sula."
> "You. Sula. What's the difference? You was there. You watched, didn't you? Me, I never would've watched." (168)

At first Nel is incredulous, but as she rushes away from Eva she begins to re-see the incident and realizes that she had watched and ". . . had been secretly proud of her calm, controlled behavior when Sula was uncontrollable." What she had believed was a calm that comes from maturity was in fact a ". . . tranquility that follows a joyful stimulation" (170). Eva had told her that she and Sula were always similar: "'Just alike. Both of you. Never was no difference between you'"

(169). She, like Sula, had been moved by this one moment of inconstancy; she and Sula had once been one in their participation and acceptance of human experience. At this point in her retrospection, Nel's "soft ball of fur" breaks and scatters in the wind; her controlled and static life dissolves into "a fine cry — long and loud. . . .":

> "All that time, all that time, I thought I was missing Jude." And the loss pressed down on her chest and came up into her throat. "We was girls together," she said as though explaining something. "O Lord, Sula," she cried, "girl, girl, girlgirlgirl." (174)

The novel closes with this mournful, belated recognition that with Sula, Nel had achieved her sense of me-ness. With Sula she had attempted to discover herself through experience, and thus, for a time, she had circumvented the survivalist confines of the Bottom. With Sula, Nel may have continued to explore her potentialities; she may have transformed her life; and if she and her community had tried to understand Sula's call, they may have responded with their own imaginative attempts toward creative action and perhaps broken the bonds of a sexist, introjected order. Instead, Nel is left with ". . . just circles and circles of sorrow" (174); and therein Morrison suggests that a synthesis of call and response cannot occur so long as all of the Bottom's inhabitants and their descendants remain trapped within a behavioral and perceptual order that denies human diversity and potential.

Chapter V

Song of Solomon: Reality and Mythos Within the Community

While Claudia in *The Bluest Eye* and Nel in *Sula* are too late to change what has happened in their lives, Milkman Dead, in Morrison's third novel, *Song of Solomon*, completes a heroic quest for an identity and place within the community. Morrison depicts Milkman in mythic terms. Not only does his story follow a cohesive pattern of miraculous birth, youth/alienation, quest, confrontation, and reintegration into community, but Morrison also infuses it with both Western and African-American myths which blend together the mundane with the magical and the factual with the fantastic. Morrison juxtaposes her own mythic variations with the "reality" of Milkman's conservative, middle-class family which, like himself and his community, is fractured by the absence of a historical or cultural identity. This juxtaposition is central to the novel in that Morrison uses myth to tie Milkman and his people to their historical and cultural past and, more important, to underscore their need for a black cultural and historical context.

The novel focuses on two morally and ethically antithetical positions, which are represented within the same black family. The father, Macon Dead II, who lives in and espouses the American Dream myth, promulgates the belief that the introjection of white capitalism's competitive, success-oriented motivations and actions are the only viable alternatives for the fulfillment and advancement of the black race. In short, Macon Dead (makin' dead) has buried whatever black identity or heritage he has in an effort to accumulate wealth and the semblance of white upper middle-class status; and thus, like blue eyes and Shirley Temple, Macon's myth distorts and dislocates the realities of black life.

Early in the novel he tells his son that there is only "one important thing you'll ever need to know. Own things. And let the things you own own other things. Then you'll own yourself and other people too" (55). Macon's manipulation of power and of people as objects not only inhibits him from establishing loving, sensitive relationships, but it also enables him to escape his own identity and heritage and, in turn, to not pass on any heritage to his own children save for his capitalist pronouncements and achievements. Consequently, for the Macon Dead family, the American Dream has replaced the memory of a black cultural heritage.

Macon's insensitivity has infected his entire family. His wife, Ruth, whom he treats abominably by periodically beating her and denying her love and sexual gratification, has withdrawn into a fantasy world seeking comfort in sleeping on her father's grave and nursing Milkman until he is eight years old. Macon's two daughters, First Corinthians and Magdalena called Lena, having received little love in their lives, regale themselves in the material trappings of middle-class ritual and convention. And because he knows no other way, Milkman, for a time, passively accepts his father's selfish code and, as a young adult, works for him in the real estate and rental business. In short, the atmosphere surrounding the Dead family hardly constitutes what one might call a loving and warm one but is, instead, cold and cruelly comical (Morrison's use of irony and hyperbole is worth noting here):

> Macon kept each member of his family awkward with fear. His hatred for his wife glittered and sparked in every word he spoke to her. The disappointment he felt in his daughters sifted down on them like ash, dulling their buttery complexions and choking the lilt out of what should have been girlish voices. Under the frozen heat of his glance they tripped over doorsills and dropped the salt cellar into the yolks of their poached eggs. The way he mangled their grace, wit, and self-esteem was the single excitement of their days. Without the tension and drama he ignited, they might not have known what to do with themselves. (10)

Macon and his family exemplify the patriarchal, nuclear family which traditionally has been a critical and stable feature in Western societies. However, the destructive undercurrents of manipulation and objectification within the Dead family symbolize the degeneration of Western values, particularly in light of the disjunctive social and economic realities within black American communities. As a consequence, the Macon Dead family, rigid with convention and construct, is left muted and emotionally drained.

But these images do not begin the novel. Instead, the opening scene presents a mandril from which Morrison develops her contrastive and transformational mythopoesis. When Milkman is born, he is the first black baby admitted to the town's white-only Mercy Hospital. He is born on the day after Robert Smith, a North Carolina Mutual Life Insurance agent, leaps to his death from the roof of Mercy. Vowing in a letter that he would ". . . take off from Mercy and fly away on [his] own wings," he attracts a crowd of "forty or fifty people" (3) who stand to watch even though it is the dead of winter. In the crowd are Ruth, pregnant with Milkman, and her two young daughters. The sight of Smith clad in his "blue silk wings" causes Ruth to drop her peck basket full of "red velvet rose petals": "Her half-grown daughters scramble about trying to catch them, while the mother moan[s] and [holds] the underside of her stomach" (5). In the midst of these images of flight, roses, and labor pains, Milkman's Aunt Pilate, sister to Macon and at this point in the text identified only as a woman singer, bursts into song about "Sugarman":

> "O Sugarman done fly away
> Sugarman done gone
> Sugarman cut across the sky
> Sugarman gone home. . . . (5)

She also appears as a prophetess predicting Milkman's birth, as she tells Ruth, "'a little bird'll be here with the morning'" (8). All of which compels the onlookers to think of this entire spectacle as "some form of worship" (6), and in a way it is, for what they and we are witnessing is a mythic enactment of heroic birth in addition to a prefigurement of Morrison's entire mythopoesis.

Traditionally, the mythic hero is born or enters into a barren region, a wasteland, and Morrison underscores this with symbols of inertia and disenfranchisement within the community. The Southside residents playfully call Mercy Hospital, No Mercy Hospital, and the street that it's located on, officially called Mains Avenue, has been renamed Not Doctor Street (formerly Doctor Street). It is so named because before his death, Ruth's father, Dr. Foster, had lived on the street. But the residents' act of mind over institutions has done little to change their social or economic status. Furthermore, the community is located in an unnamed upper Michigan city on Lake Superior. The setting is therefore both fixed and fluid, which compels its residents to remain in both enclosure and flight. The narrator comments that ". . . the longing to leave becomes acute, and a break from the area, therefore, is necessarily dream-bitten, but necessary nonetheless." However, since, as the narrator continues, ". . . those five Great Lakes which the St. Lawrence feeds with memories of the sea are themselves landlocked. . ." (163), the community endures this necessary duality of experience wherein the sea places physical restrictions upon them while continuing to symbolize the potential for renewal through motion.

It is fitting, then, that the novel opens with the image of flight as both destabilizing and as liberating. Mr. Smith's Icarus-like death and Milkman's predicted birth are marked by communal recognition and celebration, or as the narrator tells us, "it was nice and gay there for a while" (5); and indeed, we seem to be watching a scene of simple, albeit ironic, merriment. A child is "miraculously" born, a first-born male child marked by flight; his birth, as we later learn, is the result of a love potion given by Pilate to Ruth in order to bring Macon to Ruth's bed (who has been loveless for 13 years, another image of barrenness). When Macon learns of the pregnancy, he attempts, through various abortion techniques, to kill the unborn child because he believes that Ruth has had an incestuous relationship with her father.

During Milkman's childhood, he is sheltered and nurtured to an extreme; his mother breast-feeds him beyond infancy, and in doing so, she feels "like the miller's daughter—the one who sat at night in a straw-filled room, thrilled with the secret power Rumpelstilskin had given her: to see golden thread stream from her very own shuttle" (13). All of these introductory images of barrenness, celebration, subterfuge, and shelter lend a kind of simple fairytale quality to the story; and further, beyond these moments, Milkman's childhood itself has a certain vagueness to it, which is also inherent in a traditional story of the mythic hero. Myth, according to Roland Barthes, "abolish[es] the complexity of human acts, it gives them the simplicity of essences . . . , it establishes a blissful clarity: things appear to mean something by themselves" (143). And indeed, with the imposition of myth, Morrison appears to have provided a clear foundation for a traditional story of heroic quest.

But there is much that is unstable in this opening scene of mythic reenactment. Barthes claims that myth ". . . transforms history into nature" (143), and to a certain degree, Milkman's historical beginnings appear to become naturalized. However, Morrison characteristically inverts and thus undercuts these "naturalized" images, and in doing so, begins to recreate her own special mythos. Milkman is born during the winter season that symbolizes death, and the spectre of his birth is greeted by Ruth's red velvet roses which also symbolize death; but more importantly, they are artificial roses and thus suggest an impoverishment to the extreme. And finally, the most obvious (and humorous) inversion in this mythic reenactment is that Milkman is born Dead. It is a metaphor which will linger and influence much of his life, as he later says, "'You gonna do me in? My name is [Milkman], remember? I'm already Dead'" (118). Born into the community's principal family, Milkman should have nothing but silver-spoon success in his life; instead, he senses his deadness at the early age of four. When he discovers that "only birds and airplanes [can] fly" (9), he becomes bereft of all imagination. If anything, Milkman is born into and lives an entirely unnatural existence; his life is grounded from the very beginning by distortion and disaffection. The remainder of the novel encompasses Milkman's attempts to overcome his own disaffec-

tion, to learn to fly (again), and thus to transcend the unbliss-
ful inauthenticity surrounding his life.

Morrison continues her mythopoesis in the structural
multiplicity that is apparent in the novel's early stages. These
shifting and multiple perspectives serve to dramatize the
limitations of the heroic myth as merely an existential abstrac-
tion. Surrounding Milkman are other characters who provide
guidance and example and thereby confirm Milkman's
centrality in the text; but often the isolation and the alienation
that he experiences parallel other characters' lives. Therefore,
Morrison attempts to adapt the heroic quest and its outcome to
both individual and collective levels within a black historical
context.

For instance, the disaffection which Milkman experiences in
his adult life is, in some ways, foreshadowed by his mother.
Ruth has lived a "baby doll" existence (197), she has been
made weak and passive by the "affectionate elegance" (12) of
her father's class-conscious upbringing, and she has been
rendered invisible and inconsequential by her boorish and
dominating husband. She has, in short, lived her life in
service to the patriarchal order. She finds meaning and
presence in her life through a watermark on the dining room
table. Throughout her father's life, it was there that a bowl of
"fresh flowers had stood. Every day." Now, she regards the
stain as "a mooring, a checkpoint, some stable visual object
that assure[s] her that the world [is] still there . . . that she [is]
alive somewhere" (11).

Loveless and invisible, Ruth also clings selfishly to Milkman,
using him, like the watermark, as a measure of personal
stability while realizing that "her son [has] never been a
person to her, a separate real person. He [has] always been a
passion" (131). Milkman is "her single triumph," and her
personal affrontery to a world that has given her neither love
nor purpose. The used has necessarily become the user; first
in her father and later in Milkman, she lives her life in the
memory and passion of another's gaze.

In perhaps the most telling scene, the entire family's torpid
position is made analogous to their touring car. Each Sunday,
Macon takes his family for a Sunday drive and although "it [is]

a less ambitious ritual for Ruth . . . , [it is] a way, nevertheless, for her to display her family." For Macon, this ritual is "much too important for [him] to enjoy" (31). Ironically, however, what appears as a dignified, stately ritual for the Dead family is seen with "a whole lot of amusement" (32) by some community members. Again, the community's playfulness serves to identify incongruity in their midst. For the Dead family, the "wide green Packard" has no practical function beyond the self-serving ritual of familial exposition:

> [Macon] hailed no one and no one hailed him. There was never a sudden braking and backing up to shout or laugh with a friend. No beer bottles or ice cream cones poked from the open windows. Nor did a baby boy stand up to pee out of them. He never let rain fall on it if he could help it and he walked to Sonny's Shop—taking the car out only on these occasions. (32)

To the community, then, "the Packard [has] no real lived life at all. So they [call] it Macon Dead's hearse" (32).

Increasingly, as Milkman matures, he feels these "burdens" (31) of the family's unsubstantial rituals. He feels a desire, a "concentration on things behind him," and senses that there is "no future to be had" (35). The cultural deadness of his family and the anger and isolation of his home provide the impetus for liberation. Milkman's second stage of growth, the period of alienation and desire for understanding, reflect the ordering principal behind the mythic pattern. He begins to acknowledge a vague yearning for wholeness in his otherwise other-directed existence. At the age of twelve, he befriends a more worldly boy, Guitar, who takes "him to the woman who [has] as much to do with his future as she [has] his past" (35).

Long since barred from the respectable Macon Dead family, Pilate, her daughter, Reba, and Reba's daughter, Hagar, emerge at an important juncture in the text, for they provide a contrary and disruptive influence in the folk image that they project to Milkman. His perceptions of Pilate, formed as they are by Macon who thinks of his sister as a "snake" (54), by townspeople who identify her as "ugly, dirty, poor, drunk," and by "sixth-grade schoolmates" who subsequently tease him about his "queer aunt" (37), become less other-directed when he first meets her.

Pilate and her family subsist in materially impoverished surroundings, making and selling bootleg wine, but Milkman sees that Pilate, while "she [is] anything but pretty" (37), is neither dirty nor drunk. She presents herself to the boys as she appears in the beginning of the novel with the presence of strength, confidence, and good humor. She is the archetypal, black folk singer and oral storyteller whose personal stories give shape to a collective consciousness.

To the two young boys, her presence is magical and mysterious, and as the odor of pine and fermenting wine sends them into "a pleasant semi-stupor" (46), Pilate entrances the boys with a partial story of her life:

> "Hadn't been for your daddy, I wouldn't be here today. I would have died in the womb. And died again in the woods. Those woods and the dark would have surely killed me. But he saved me and here I am boiling eggs. Our papa was dead, you see. They blew him five feet up into the air. He was sitting on his fence waiting for 'em and they snuck up from behind and blew him five feet into the air. So when we left Circe's big house we didn't have no place to go, so we just walked around and lived in them woods. . . . And talking about dark! You think dark is just one color, but it ain't. There're five or six kinds of black. Some silky, some woolly. Some just empty. Some like fingers. And it don't stay still. It moves and changes from one kind of black to another." (40)

Encapsulated into Pilate's untethered story is the familiar violence, degradation, and victimization that surround black life. The woods and the darkness convey the fear, loneliness, and alienation of black reality, but Pilate also testifies to the courage and self-sufficiency that she and Macon demonstrated and, even though they now travel diametrically opposing paths, they continue to demonstrate.

As Pilate continues to testify, it is Guitar and not Milkman who responds with questions about her father, her father's farm, its location, and the year of Pilate's and Macon's untimely flight. But characteristic of an oral storyteller, Pilate relates events to events and moment to moments which intersect with a pulsing poetic quality that transforms historical fact into a felt experience. When Guitar asks, "'What year?'", Pilate responds, "'The year they shot them Irish people down in the streets. Was a good year for guns and gravediggers'"

(42). Pilate's poetic valences of personal history collide with Guitar's wordly desire for a sanitized, concrete version of events, and as such, Pilate's other-wordliness, her home and her lifestyle embody a funkiness far removed and yet not removed from the realities of the two boys' lives.

One aspect to Morrison's work which seems most apparent is the desire to establish and maintain a black cultural heritage in the face of the homogenizing effects of late capitalism. Each of her novels pinpoints historical moments of disruption and transformation in that heritage. Both *The Bluest Eye* and *Sula* focus primarily on the 1940's when heavy black migrations to the cities precipitated black incorporation into modern American capitalism. In *Song of Solomon*, this incorporation seems complete as the novel's central positioning of a black bourgeois family suggests. For Macon Dead, late capitalism and its socializing effects have replaced the rural, Southern past and he has therefore made it inaccessible to his children.

The pervasive influence of late capitalism is a signpost to repression and desire for the Dead family; but, in Aunt Pilate, they also share a common thread—desperately stretched thin—to Pilate's embodiment of a black heritage. This explains why on a sensual level Milkman is able to recognize the folk heritage surrounding Pilate and her home:

> . . . it was the first time in his life that he remembered being completely happy. . . . He was sitting comfortably in the notorious wine house; he was surrounded by women who seemed to enjoy him and who laughed out loud. And he was in love. No wonder his father was afraid of them. (47)

Milkman sees a family who, unlike his own, lives their lives simply: "They ate what they had or came across or had a craving for" (29). The three women treat him with generosity, kindness, and love; and, as he thinks, "all of them [have] a guileless look about them. . ." (46). He and we have entered into what appears to be a social utopia, an alternative world of blissful clarity where difference articulates a form of liberation from the predictable and reified world of Macon Dead.

Even Macon himself, in spite of his objection to Pilate's difference, feels liberated as he one night walks past the wine house and hears the women singing. He, too, "surrender[s] to the sound. . ." and feels "himself softening under the weight of memory and music. . ." (29-30) Pilate's world is cyclical, expansive, and alluring to anyone who comes in contact with it. Instead of repressing the past, she carries it with her in the form of songs and stories and synthesizes it with the present. Her past softens and liberates others because she evokes and embodies a collective (un)consciousness which manifests itself in what the narrator calls, "a deep concern for and about human relationships" (150). Pilate's folk culture may appear antithetical to the Macon Dead family, but its liberating song pulses through their lives and through the lives of the entire community. Consciously, as Macon says the three are "'just like common street women'" (20), but intuitively, he and the community feel the signficance of their collective difference.

On the surface, however, both families remain split apart by their two modes of self-awareness, and this point of devisiveness places Milkman in an alienated position of desire and vacillation. Identity for Pilate is found in a connective energy, one that evokes a living heritage through story and song. Macon teaches his son that identity can only be found in the future, in his linear vision to "own things," "own people," and therefore "own yourself." He wishes to escape the past because it has, for him, no materially functional purpose.

Displaced between these two visions, Milkman chooses not to choose. Rather than attaching himself to any belief or commitment and acting from any set of principles, Milkman only reacts, self-consciously and indifferently, to whatever transpires about him. As he grows older, he passively submits to being his father's lackey, collecting rents, keeping the books. His passive position is physically manifested in his deformed gait. Since one of his legs is shorter than the other, he limps, and he attempts to disguise his defect with "an affected walk, the strut of a very young man trying to appear more sohpisticated than he [is]" (62).

Moreover, he seldom accepts responsibility for his actions and when he does, it is only to demonstrate his own self-righteousness. For instance, when he strikes his father for humiliating his mother, he does so because he believes himself to be "wide-spirited and generous enough" (69) to do so. To prove that he is not a bad man, Macon tells Milkman that he had seen Ruth naked and kissing her deceased father. Macon, in his own distorted way, wishes to justify his continued humiliation of Ruth, and ironically his continued support for his wife; as he believes, there is "'nothing to do but kill a woman like that'" (74).

But instead of making Milkman understand his behavior, Macon, in exposing the reason for his loveless marriage, inadvertently prompts a shocked Milkman into realizing that he "never . . . thought of his mother as a person, a separate individual, with a life apart from allowing or interfering with his own'" (75). Milkman vaguely begins to realize that his reactions, be they positive or negative, are haphazard and uninformed; he had interfered in his parents' lives as a self-serving gesture without understanding that, as the narrator says, "it would change nothing between his parents" (68).

At this point in the narrative, Milkman sees himself as lacking coherence, "a coming together of the features into a total self" (70). Still, he wishes to shrug off the distortions in his life and family. And as the narrative moves quickly over the 31 years of Milkman's life, he concludes that "above all he want[s] to escape. . ." from all that he knows. Feeling "put upon" (120) by his family, Milkman yearns for some identity separate from what he considers his family's abnormalities.

Perhaps this is why he continues to be drawn to the winehouse; he finds relief and escape from his tentative self and from his rigidly dispassionate home. But as the narrator says, he is "like a man peeping around a corner . . . trying to make up his mind whether to go forward or to turn back" (70). He is not anymore committed to Pilate's world than to his parents. He effectively uses Pilate's family in the same way his mother used him, as a way of extracting some shred of identity in the midst of his alienation:

> His visits to the wine house seemed . . . an extension of the love he had come to expect from his mother. . . . they had accepted him without question and with all the ease in the world. They took him seriously too. Asked him questions and thought all his responses to things were important enough to laugh at or quarrel with him about. (79)

When he visits Pilate's home, Milkman does not feel burdened by what he is told or by other's expectations of him. And it is clear that he assumes a central position in the house which brings with it his own sense of self-importance. Since, at the wine house, he does not have "to think or be or do something" about any aspect of his life, his hosts unintentionally support his indifference or what the narrator calls his "lazy righteousness" (120).

To further complicate his involvement with the family, he and Hagar become sexually attracted to each other, and at the respective ages of seventeen and twenty-two, they consummate the relationship. For the first three years, Milkman is delighted by the affair especially since, whenever he appears, she is "all smiles and welcome." After fourteen years, however, the attraction has diminished for Milkman. His indifference is heightened in direct proportion to Hagar's increasingly possessive love, and both attitudes have destructive potential.

The narrator comments that "Milkman [has] stretched his carefree boyhood out for thirty-one years. Hagar [is] thirty-six-and nervous" (98). He feels that "there [is] no excitement, no galloping blood in his neck or his heart at the thought of her" (91). She looks to him for a definitive commitment. What Milkman does give her is a cold, business-like rejection letter thanking her for all the years of happiness. Obviously Milkman has not developed any kind of "deep concern for and about human relationships." He yearns instead to run away in narcissistic flight beyond his increasingly enclosed, static existence. For her part, Hagar responds with a stalking desire to kill Milkman whose life ironically becomes further enclosed as he tries to avoid and hide from her.

But what of Hagar's fate? As we later learn, Milkman's mixture of frustration, isolation, and alienation become the impetus for his open motion toward independence and eventually to collective engagement. Any comparable sensations send Hagar "spinning into a bright blue place where the air [is] thin" (99). Both the presence and absence of Milkman have hurled her into a misdirected flight away from any self-identity or visioned responsibility to the self. Her identity has become fully subsumed in Milkman's gaze. Later in the novel, she worries, as she lays dying, that, like Pecola Breedlove, she has been unacceptable to Milkman because she does not have the "'penny-colored hair,' 'lemon-colored skin,' and 'gray-blue eyes'" (319) that he likes.

Early in the novel a pattern develops which shows that women exist for males as mere operatives. Mothers and lovers live for and linger in the presence and absence of dead fathers, Dead husbands, and indifferent male lovers. They appear, like Milkman, as passive victims, they convey understanding and guidance, and even, like Pilate, they appear as free-flyers who project a self-sustaining image. But never does their alienation, their awareness, or their apparent freedom lead to a positive engagement with the community. They remain decentered, disengaged, and are even killed off in the text. No matter how similar they appear, they lack Milkman's possibilities, they play no central role, their dreams, if they have them at all, remain unfulfilled until the male hero fulfills them. As Simone de Beauvoir says of women in her *The Second Sex*, the women in *Song of Solomon* "still dream through the dreams of men" (161). Thus, Morrison's use of multiple, parallel perspectives does not entirely resolve the male-centered mythic bias in the novel.

Of course Milkman does appear as a surrogate for others, including women. He is portrayed as one who attempts to find a self and place within a black cultural context, and in doing so, he can inspire and lead others. He can, in short, become a model for others to emulate. But in spite of parallel perspectives and collective identities in *Song of Solomon*, the traditional male hero remains the focus in the story, and with it remains the apparent active/passive stereotype of male mastery over the female, which itself is deeply rooted in traditional mythic structure. In the end, women cannot fully live and know the meaning of Milkman's quest as he finally does. As we shall see, Milkman is finally reconciled with his forefathers; conversely, the same sense of history is never made available to women.

This lack of full and equal participation in heroic models of myth and history is clearly and consciously illustrated through the character of Pilate. Like Sula's, Pilate's story indicates that she possesses the essences of the existential male hero. The first years of Pilate's life are peaceful and almost idyllic,; she and her father and brother live and prosper on their farm in Pennsylvania until the children witness the murder of their father by a powerful white family in a land-grab scheme. Six days later, the two homeless orphans find refuge with Circe who works in a white family's mansion.

After two weeks of hiding and boredom, Pilate and Macon, Jr., set out for Virginia, "where Macon believe[s] they [have] people" (168). Soon afterward, she and Macon separate after Macon kills an old, white man when the frightened Macon stumbles upon him in a cave. In the cave, Macon finds three bags of gold, but Pilate, fearful of being accused of both murder and theft, insists that they leave the gold buried. The two children fight and the knife-wielding Pilate chases Macon from the cave. When Macon returns three days later, both Pilate and the gold are gone.

Now on her own, Pilate continues on her journey to Virginia, and on her way, she is first taken in by a preacher's family. At school, she develops a love for geography and is given a geography book by her teacher. She yearns to travel about and so, with only her geography book, she joins with migrant workers, and while she never finds her relations, she lives with a man on an isolated island off the coast of Virginia, and with him conceives her daughter, Reba. But Pilate refuses to marry the man and sets out again for Pennsylvania to retrieve what she thinks are the murdered old man's bones. She begins "the wandering life that she [keeps] up for the next twenty-some-odd years, and stop[s] only after Reba [has] a baby" (148). Thereafter, she seeks out and finds her brother, believing that "Hagar needed family, people, a life very different from what she and Reba could offer. . ." (151). Hagar, as she grows older, prefers a more organized, more conventional lifestyle, which Pilate correctly assumes and hopes Macon can provide.

This is Pilate's life-history. She has overcome great odds and obstacles; she has been a woman alone who raises and provides for a family, and all the while, she lives the life of an archetypal "running man" whose vision of progress is encom-

passed in the physical actualizations of her geography book.
But unlike the "running man" of history, Pilate does not fly
away from responsibility; hers is a desired flight toward a
communal consciousness, toward, as the narrator says, an
"alien's compassion for troubled people" (150), which itself
transcends the world's meanness and selfishness.

Another aspect which significantly forms her life is yet
another of Morrison's magical infusions. Pilate has no navel.
As a child, she encounters a root woman who tells her what a
navel is for: "'It's for . . . it's for people who were born
natural'" (144). Throughout the novel, Pilate embodies the
spiritual resources of African-American folk traditions, and as
such, she appears as a kind of supernatural character, an earth
mother, a voodoo priestess and conjour, a mythical storyteller.
But in the everyday world, her lack of a navel marks her as
unnatural, and as word spreads of it, she becomes unwelcome
and/or isolated in any community. Her refusal to marry her
lover is also a consequence of her lack; she is afraid that she
cannot "hide her stomach from a husband forever" (147). And
thus, her transmittal of a community spirit remains impeded.
Her world is both large and marginal. It is large in that her
vision encompasses all that is good and right and true in
human affairs. It is marginal in that it includes only her
immediate family and her father's ghost:

> It isolated her. Already without family, she was further isolated from
> her people, for except for the relative bliss on the island, every other
> resource was denied her: partnership in marriage, confessional friend-
> ship, and communal religion. Men frowned, women whispered and
> shoved their children behind them. (149)

Even so, as she hovers about the fringe, Pilate demonstrates
her strength and her desire to both persevere and preserve
her vision. After being initiated into the cruelties of the white
world and into the insensitivities of her own black world,
Pilate chooses to build a world of her own:

> Although she was hampered by huge ignorances, but not in any way
> unintelligent, when she realized what her situation in the world was
> and would probably always be, she threw away every assumption she
> had learned and began at zero. First off, she cut her hair. That was

one thing she didn't want to think about anymore. Then she tackled
the problem of trying to decide how she wanted to live and what was
valuable to her. (149)

The symbolism of cutting her hair and the definitive establishment of her position should enable Pilate to both emulate
and disarm the androcentric myth and should allow her the
freedom and connection to fully develop and perpetuate her
own vital community. But even within her own family, Pilate
is unable to transmit her strength and vision. It is true that
Pilate's vision is rooted in rural, Southern society and such a
utopian vision in its totality is clearly in opposition to an
urban, late capitalistic society.   But Morrison does not
unequivocally valorize the agrarian social mode as an obvious
alternative or answer to a Dead world. It, too, has its imper-
fections ironically because Pilate's utopian vision of love,
generosity, and a "concern for and about human relationships" are not adequately sustaining features in a pragmatic
society conditioned for acquisition and consumption.   Thus,
while Hagar has been showered with love and concern all her
life, she has actually become damaged by such excessive and
concentrated affection in that she has no inner strength to
withstand either a capitalist society or her unrequited relationship with Milkman.

But ultimately, it is Pilate's vision, placed as it is in opposition and isolation, that lends an unstable and emphemeral
quality and status to her family.   And above all, it demonstrates that while Pilate's marginality allows her the freedom
to act as a guide figure and thus gives her the opportunity to
disarm the androcentric myth, she cannot do so because she
lacks a full recognition and understanding of what has
transpired during her life, during her own "quest." Morrison
clearly indicates that in spite of their strength, courage,
intuition, and knowledge, women, like Pilate or Sula, have
been, throughout history, locked out of a fully integrated myth
in which they are central and in which they can connect to
and transmit a regenerative legacy, and therefore make themselves, and those around them, whole.   The myth of heroism
allows women to assist in and benefit from the quest for a self

and place within the community, but it does not allow for origination; it is historically dictated in a patriarchal society, then, that Milkman play the central role in the mythic quest.

Milkman appears as a surrogate for his father's greed, and thus, after he and Guitar fail the first time to find Pilate's gold, Milkman decides to travel alone to Danville, Pennsylvania, because, as he says, "'Daddy thinks the stuff is still in the cave'" (222). But Milkman also has an ulterior motive; he believes that Pilate's gold will set him free from his "real life." As he takes his first airplane flight, he begins to make an unconscious connection to his aerial beginnings:

> This one time he wanted to go solo. In the air, away from real life, he felt free, but on the ground, when he talked to Guitar just before he left, the wings of all those other people's nightmares flapped in his face and constrained him. (222)

Milkman seeks freedom from all those whom he believes have treated him "like a garbage pail," dumping into him all of their "actions and hatreds" (120). But while Milkman wishes to deny the obvious, those characters surrounding him reveal to him and the reader just how detached and distorted Milkman has become. Both Milkman and Guitar represent two reactions and two alternatives to their distortion. While Milkman tentatively identifies with his father's middle-class ideology, Guitar embodies the displaced rural Southerner whose alienation, unlike Milkman's, is ensconced in racial hatred. Rather than pursue what will ultimately be Milkman's ameliorative flight toward tradition and ideals, Guitar chooses instead to right social wrongs with acts of vengeance against the dominant culture.

His position is a reaction to the primal trauma of his life when, as a boy, his father is cut in half in a sawmill accident and as recompense, his mother willingly accepts forty dollars from the white owner. His perceptions of his mother's moral cowardice and betrayal convince Guitar that his commitment to and love of black people must find its expression in hateful aggression. Guitar becomes obsessed with his disaffection to the degree that he actively participates in a secret society known as the "Seven Days." Theirs is a mission of retribution.

Whenever black people are injured or killed, they respond by randomly killing white people.

The discovery of Guitar's involvement in the Seven Days brings the reader full circle to the text's original scene. Robert Smith was himself a member of the Days and Guitar was a witness to his flightless death. Like Smith, Guitar's vision of violence begetting violence keeps him on a flightless path until he is driven to madness by his own obsession for Pilate's gold. His ideology proves just as inadequate as Macon Dead's acculturated vision. However, like his father's corpse, Guitar is a split subject. While he espouses his single-minded doctrine, he nonetheless appears as Milkman's alter-ego whose social perceptions seem more correctly fixed than Milkman's; and thus, coupled with his communal Southern background and his "slow smile of recognition" (49) toward Pilate's folk world, Guitar provides an antithetically connective energy in Milkman's search for self and place.

Guitar accurately identifies Milkman's disconnection, his lack of a cultural heritage, when he tells him that not only would Milkman not live in a place like Montgomery, Alabama, he is "'A man that can't live there.'" Guitar also makes Milkman recognize that he accepts only limited responsibility for his life and for the lives around him. He is "'not a serious person'" (104), Guitar tells him; he is merely an egg, Guitar says, whose shell needs to be broken.

In one other scene, Guitar makes Milkman analogous to a male peacock. When Milkman asks him why the peacock can't fly, Guitar tells him, "'Too much tail. All that jewelry weighs it down. Like vanity. Can't nobody fly with all that shit. Wanna fly, you got to give up the shit that weighs you down'" (179-80). Of course both characters are weighed down by their racial rootlessness—one displaced, the other detached. But Guitar, in spite of his deadly motivations, is able to more fully articulate and impress his alienation upon Milkman who would otherwise want, as the narrator says, ". . . to know as little as possible, to feel only enough to get through the day amiably. . ." (181).

The "real life" of Guitar and of Milkman's family are mirrors to Milkman, and in spite of his resistance, they reveal to him his true identity. When Milkman learns that Corinthians is dating an unsavory character, he condescendingly assumes he has "Corinthians' welfare at heart" (216) by telling his father about the affair. He takes for granted that he can take an approving or disapproving attitude. But his sister Lena reveals to her brother that he has no legitimate right, particularly in light of his uncaring, noncommital behavior, to assume a patriarchal role:

> "When did you get the *right* to decide our lives?"
> "I'll tell you where. From that hog's gut that hangs down between your legs. Well, let me tell you something, baby brother: you will need more than that. I don't know where you will get it or who will give it to you, but mark my words, you need more than that." (217)

Lena identifies Milkman's disconnection from self and place. He has lived an externalized existence; he grasps for those prescribed social codes—partying, womanizing, male-domineering—which may help to mask and assuage his insecure, unformed self. Since those surrounding him see through his masks, Milkman seeks, through Pilate's gold, a more permanent mask; but as he returns to his ancestors' world, he slowly begins to understand that culturally mythic connections prevail over his subjectively skewed perceptions.

From the beginning, Milkman's story has been infused with irony, paradox, and contradiction. Part Two of the novel continues this cycle. It blissfully begins with a synopsis of the Hansel and Gretel story supplanting gingerbread for Pilate's gold. But like the original tale of Milkman's magical birth, his actual journey will never appear as a simple, harmless fairytale. Throughout the novel, contradictions such as these reflect the divisiveness of Milkman's mind and situation. In his search for a new life, he is consciously driven by a simple desire for open motion, while at the same time, he is pulled away from such simplicity by a subconscious attachment to the complexities of an unexplored past which both his father and Pilate have partially shared with him.

When Milkman first visits with older residents of Danville, he is enticed by their stories depicting Macon Dead, Sr., as a superhuman figure. To the old men of the village, Macon, Sr., represents the ideal figure who, as an ex-slave, overcame seemingly insurmountable odds in creating his flourishing, rich farm. He was the American Adam who, unlike his son, embodied a self-reliance that did not exploit and benefit from the misfortune of others. Macon, Sr., was "head and shoulders above it all," the old men tell Milkman, and his death, ". . . was the beginning of their own dying. . ." (237). Caught up in the excitement of their stories, Milkman continues the myth and delights his audience with stories of his father's "successes."

At this point, Milkman feels another surge of self-righteousness. He wishes to avenge his grandfather's death by finding the gold, and he grows "fierce with pride" (238) as he prepares for his search. The irony here is apparent; the freedom he seeks in the gold has been replaced by a sudden "heroic" urge. But as with Lena's scathing observations, the fragmented Milkman lacks any sort of experience to make him qualify for the role. And many of the scenes which follow reinforce this inversion.

The townspeople direct Milkman to the Butler plantation, home of the now deceased white people responsible for his grandfather's death. Once he enters the dilapidated, decaying mansion, his quest assumes truly mythic proportions in that he discovers the ancient Circe still residing there, now approximately 175 years old, and waiting specifically for him. Circe stands guard to the entrance into Milkman's ancestral past. And like an Aeneas or a Ulysses, Milkman must establish direct contact with this past before he can form a path to the future. Circe tells Milkman the real names of his grandparents—Jake and Sing—and that Shalimar, Virginia is their original birthplace. Earlier we learned that Macon, Sr., had been misnamed when he was inducted into the Union army. By learning their true names and origin, Milkman has unconsciously begun his quest for self and place, for beneath their names and origins lay his connection to not only a personal heritage but to a deeper vein of black history and myth.

Circe also directs Milkman to the cave holding the gold. Milkman's appearance in the wilderness is significant in its ironic juxtapositions. Not only is Milkman out of his element, clumsy and obtuse as he stumbles about the woods, disconnected from his grandfather's natural world, but Milkman also appears as an unworthy, even unsavory character when, in the midst of archetypal images of cave and rebirth, he "smells money"; "there was nothing like it in the world" (253). Milkman finds no gold or anything else in the cave, and in the end, he is comically chased from it by its resident bats.

Even though he reemerges from the woods shaking from hunger and thirst, his clothes tattered, his watch broken in this timeless world, he returns to town foolishly convinced that the gold must still be in Virginia. Milkman's failed initiation prompts him to shed his heroic compulsions and return to his more pragmatic belief that, as he resolves, "he want[s] the gold because it [is] gold. . ." (260), and because the search for it continues his sense of freedom and open motion. But even this notion is undercut when, at the end of the scene, the narrator appropriately reminds us that Milkman is merely following in Pilate's "tracks" (261).

But if Milkman is comically ill-prepared for his personal rebirth in Danville, he is seriously ill-equipped for his encounter with the communal primitivism of Shalimar. Here Milkman enters a mystical, magical territory fraught with both dangers and delights. Because Shalimar has no bus or train depot, Milkman buys a car, and on his way through the South, he is buoyed by the "southern hospitality": ". . . the Negroes were as pleasant, wide-spirited, and self-contained as could be." But when Milkman finally happens upon Solomon's General Store his first meeting with the townsmen suggests that his notions about the South have been, like all of his perceptions, naively and compulsively formed.

In talking to them, Milkman learns that Guitar has unexpectedly arrived in Shalimar and has been looking for him. Guitar's presence fills Milkman with an uncertain fear but, for the moment, his main concern is the hostility he senses from the townsfolk. "What was all the hostility for?" Milkman wonders. ". . . they behaved as if they'd been insulted" (268-69). Without realizing it himself, Milkman's very presence has offended the townsfolk. This "city Negro," with his fancy clothes and brusque manner, appears to them as just another arrogant white man:

> [Milkman] hadn't found them fit enough or good enough to want to
> know their names, and believed himself too good to tell them his.
> They looked at his skin and saw it was as black as theirs, but they knew
> he had the heart of the white men who came to pick them up in the
> trucks when they needed anonymous, faceless laborers. (269)

While Milkman's "white" appearance underscores his racial rootlessness, the contrast between him and the townspeople also suggests that different values are associated with black urban and rural culture. To these people, his materially endowed superior airs are not adequate to justify his existence as a black man; Milkman must prove himself in the traditionally physical struggle with other men. Forced into taking a stand, Milkman beats another man in a fist and knife fight. For the first time in his life, Milkman makes a kind of commitment; his solo entrance into the rural South and this violent confrontation have emboldened him to take risks, to, as he thinks, "stop evading things, sliding through, over, and around difficulties" (274).

His exposure to the rural South and Shalimar also forces him to begin taking a more realistic view of the world around him. Throughout the South he had met people who were "nice to him, generous, helpful." The men in Shalimar, however, were "some of the meanest unhung niggers in the world" (273). Perhaps, as he thinks, the people on his journey had been "just curious and amused." In truth, Milkman "hadn't stayed in any place long enough to find out" (279), which analogously sums up the whole of Milkman's life. The basic humanness of Shalimar, of Pilate, and even of Guitar, their unpretentious emotions, their struggles for survival, are completely alien to Milkman, blocked out by a lifetime of material and emotional isolation. He has measured self-esteem in gold and in the "hero worship" (273) associated with material success. In Shalimar, however, the skills to measure self-worth involve those raw emotions and survival skills.

Milkman has entered into an almost primeval world, a world that is fast disappearing against the onslaught of a Dead world. It is a world that still considers human beings to be on equal footing with one another, where "not his money, his car, his father's reputation, his suit, or his shoes. . ." will help him;

"where all a man had was what he was born with, or had to learn to use. . ." (280). These realizations are more firmly impressed upon him when he joins the townsmen on a bobcat hunt. The hunt, in the tradition of Faulkner's *The Bear*, functions on three different levels. On the literal level, the men successfully kill, and eventually eat, a bobcat. On another level, Milkman is almost strangled to death by Guitar, who has been following him in hopes of retrieving the never-found gold. Finally, Milkman is hunting for a self free from personal inhibition and social pretention. In the shrouded forest, a backdrop to his bewildered psyche, Milkman realizes that he has permitted the American Dream myth to devalue his senses and block out his natural ability to be a loving, empathetic human being:

> Now it seemed to him that he was always saying or thinking that he didn't deserve some bad luck, or some bad treatment from others. He'd told Guitar that he didn't "deserve" his family's dependence, hatred, or whatever. That he didn't even "deserve" to hear all the misery and mutual accusations his parents unloaded on him. But why shouldn't his parents tell him their personal problems? If not him, then who?
>
> Apparently he thought he deserved only to be loved—from a distance, though—and given what he wanted. And in return he would be . . . what? Pleasant? Generous? Maybe all he was really saying was: I am not responsible for your pain; share your happiness with me but not your unhappiness. (280)

In the solitary wilderness of the woods, Milkman feels compelled to confront his essential identity, and his epiphany is the impetus for personal change and transcendence. But Morrison carefully avoids keeping Milkman at merely an existential plane. Hunting as the traditional symbol for brotherhood and belonging frames and underscores Milkman's sudden awakening to his essential connection to other people.

Furthermore, the wilderness, Milkman thinks, contains a language that is "before language." "Language in the time when men and animals did talk to one another . . . , when a tiger and a man could share the same tree" (281). In this spirit of collective identity, Milkman feels "a sudden rush of affection" and connection toward everyone he has known because, like him, he realizes that, in being forced to live unnatural lives, they, too, have been "maimed" and "scarred" (282). Thus, like Pilate, Guitar, and his father, they all have been conditioned to live in isolation, alienation and denial.

Milkman now feels as if he truly understands the reasons for Guitar's alienation and hatred. Moments later, however, Milkman's idealistic reverie is ironically and abruptly halted when Guitar ambushes Milkman from behind and nearly succeeds in strangling him to death before being frightened away by a shotgun blast. Ambiguity appears to surround the ironic undercutting of this scene. Guitar's realistic entrance into Milkman's mythic initiation might suggest that his mind continues to be filled with romantic notions about the meaning of his quest. But when Milkman returns to the camp and tells the other hunters that he was "'scared to death,'" his fear turns to laughter; "he [finds] himself exhilarated by simply walking the earth" (284). He no longer limps, and unlike his earlier contrary impressions of the South and Shalimar, his new-found idealism appears secure, while at the same time he no longer fears himself or the unknown. His mythic initiation and transformation coupled with his fearlessly empathic appraisal of Guitar implies that Milkman is now able to mediate between both myth and reality. As his initiation signifies, it is the myth of brotherhood and belonging which ultimately springs from and iluminates reality.

When Milkman first arrived in Shalimar, he had heard the children singing the Song of Solomon, "that old blues song Pilate sang all the time: 'O Sugarman don't leave me here,' except the children [sing] 'Solomon don't leave me here'" (303). The song is the clue to Milkman's family history, but more significantly, it also becomes for him an affirmation for kinship and community. As he more carefully listens to the song again, Milkman is finally able to piece together his genealogy. Symbols of flying permeate the children's ritual while, as they sing, one child "turn[s] around like an airplane" (267). And as they sing, Milkman listens to them recount the flight from slavery of his grandfather's father, Solomon or Shalimar, back to the freedom of his African homeland. The song is both a variant of the flying African folktales and of the Icarus tale. Solomon literally flies off with his infant son, Jake, leaving behind his wife, Ryna, and some twenty other children. Susan Byrd, cousin to Jake's wife, Sing, confirms to Milkman the magical tale behind the song:

> "No, I mean flew. . . . He was flying. He flew. You know like a bird. Just stood up in the fields one day, ran up some hill, spun around a couple of times, and was lifted up in the air." (326)

But, as Susan continues, Solomon "'brushed too close to a tree and the baby slipped out of his arms'" (327), so that Jake, too, was left behind which signaled the long rupture in his family's history.

We have once again come full circle in the novel. From the beginning, all images and scenes of flight have ended either in death, disillusion, or desertion. Robert Smith, driven to madness and to an "artifical" flight, had wished to free himself from the death and distortion of the Seven Days. Milkman's failed flight for gold violates the principle of responsibility to others, and is especially destructive to Hagar who later dies alone and inconsolate. And Solomon's flight, while freeing him to return to his homeland, results in the abandonment of family and friends. These types of absolute freedoms through flight are problematic because they involve the denial of personal and social bonds.

But within these negative images of flight lies a significant contradiction. The flights of Smith, Milkman, and Solomon are not, like Icarus', the result of *hubris* and the desire for an impossible kind of freedom. Instead, each character has "flown" to escape a particular brand of oppression and thus, Morrison has reconstructed the myth to reveal its inherent limitations within black culture and has shown the essential conflict it presents for both individual and community.

Milkman's flight has restored his sense of community because not only does the myth open out his family's history but, as he later realizes, to recover names was a way to pierce the invisibility that history had imposed on them:

> He read the road signs with interest now, wondering what lay beneath the names. The Algonquins had named the territory he lived in Great War, *michi gami*. How many dead lives and fading memories were buried in and beneath the names of the places in this country. Under

> the recorded names were other names, just as "Macon Dead," recorded
> for all time in some dusty file, hid from view the real names of people,
> places, and things. Names that had meaning. No wonder Pilate put
> hers in her ear. When you know your name, you should hang on to it,
> for unless it is noted down and remembered, it will die when you do.
> (333)

Milkman returns to the Southside to tell Pilate the good news of these rediscovered names and to correct her misconceptions about them. Pilate's mother died in childbirth and her name was never revealed to Pilate. "Sing, Sing" is not her father's request to sing, but a call to his wife. "You just can't fly on off and leave a body" is not simply a moral precept, but her father's plea to bury his bones which she unknowingly has carried with her for all these years.

But Milkman is not at first given his opportunity. Pilate breaks "a wet green bottle over his head" (335) and locks him in her cellar. Filled with exuberance, Milkman had come home with the vision of Solomon as a hero and model: "'He didn't need no airplane. He just took off; got fed up. *All the way up!* No more cotton! No more bales! No more orders! No more shit! He flew, baby'" (332). Milkman identifies with Solomon which fuels his own desire for personal identity and independence, for a freedom that transcends his own blighted world. However, Pilate's interposition furthers the mythic contradiction because she rightly blames Milkman for Hagar's death; like Solomon, he had flown off and left a body.

In the cellar-cave, Milkman begins to comprehend this contradiction, and by doing so, he experiences a true metamorphosis and eventual reemergence into his community. He makes the connection between his desertion of Hagar to Solomon's desertion of Ryna and the twenty-one children, as he wonders to himself, "Who looked after those twenty children? Jesus Christ, he left twenty-one children!" (336). Milkman realizes that the locus for his personal identity is inextricably linked to Pilate's principle of responsibility to others. And thus, he learns that objectification and commodification of people only serve to further his sense of distortion and alienation. When Milkman finally tells Pilate of his discoveries, the two return to Shalimar to bury her father's bones. At the burial site, Pilate is shot and killed by Guitar; the potential for Pilate to carry forth a new myth wherein Sing's legacy is traced to her descendants is forever silenced.

But paradoxically, in Pilate's death, we are left with an image of Pilate that offers the only definitive transcendence in the novel. As Milkman affirms, she is a person who "without ever leaving the ground . . . could fly" (340). Her spirit has surpassed all the other negative images of flight; she is the one character who, in spite of her physical restlessness and isolation, has been able to strike a balance and resolve the conflict between a personal and a collective consciousness. Deeply believing that "you can't fly off and leave a body," she alone and forever has lived a life of "honesty and equilibrium" (136) which had combined the best aspects of self, place, and motion.

As the novel closes, Pilate's spirit continues to soar through Milkman. As Guitar closes in on him, Milkman leaps, flying toward his "brother man," and not caring "which one of them would give up his ghost in the killing arms of his brother." In recognizing the mythic spirit of connection and commitment through Pilate's now usable past, Milkman does not fly away, he leaps in acknowledgment of personal kinship and brotherhood. He realizes that only in commitment is he free, "for now he knew what Shalimar knew: If you surrendered to the air, you could ride it" (341).

Milkman's reintegration into the community depends upon his acceptance of individual relationships which, in the end, he can only achieve through personal heroism. In choosing to "ride" toward Guitar, Milkman must take his ultimate risk which may very well end in his death, but as the novel's open-ending suggests, his flight forever sets in motion an open and necessary dialectic between a communal spirit and a factional reality.

Chapter VI

Tar Baby: The Presence and Absence of Self and Place

Toni Morrison's fourth novel, *Tar Baby* (1981), represents both a departure from her earlier novels and an extension of her previous concerns. Images of detachment, exile, and indecision pervade the novel and remain fixed presences throughout; thus, unlike *Song of Solomon*, for instance, there is a decided lack of transmutation in *Tar Baby*. Each character, in one way or another, remains disconnected from identity and place, from community and memory; and whatever past they retain remains inaccessible, held separate by dreams and dream visions. Yet, like her earlier novels, even these fixed and complex images of lack continue to reflect and express the urgency, difficulty, and, in this novel perhaps, the impossibility of preserving a generational continuity and a collective (un)consciousness within an increasingly individual, fragmented Western culture.

The setting for the novel is the tropical Carribean Isle des Chevaliers. Its name commemorates the legend that black slaves were struck blind upon first seeing the island, and that their blind descendants continue to ride horses around the hillside. The narrator infuses the island with its own collective consciousness. Here, amongst themselves, emperor butterflies talk, fish listen, champion daisy trees look serene, and voices whisper together from the island's swamp. Taken together, legend, blindness and natural cohesion become metaphors for social difference as they are contrasted with the island's white inhabitants.

Their intrusion distorts the form of freedom that is represented in the island's animated, subterranean world. The white vacationers must alter the course of the island's river in order to build "a collection of magnificent winter houses" (7). Thereafter, the island articulates its lack by being transformed into a kind of postlapsarian paradise; the monsoons cease, the trees mutter, and the swamp becomes "a shriveled fogbound oval seeping with a thick black substance that even mosquitoes [can] not live near" (8). This abduction of the island's threatening, collective consciousness provides a frame for the novel's developing dialectic between the presence of individual assertion and the absence of cultural cohesiveness.

Valerian and Margaret Street own one of the magnificent tropical winter mansions, L'Arbe de la Croix. He is a retired candy manufacturer from Philadelphia; she a former beauty queen from Maine. Sydney and Ondine Childs are their black servants. Jadine Childs is their orphaned niece whose Sorbonne education has been funded by Valerian. Together, they create a climate of outward calm and stability where, as the narrator notes, "almost nothing [is] askew and the few things that [are have] charm" (9). Valerian, as his imperial name implies, is particularly intent upon asserting a ritualized control over his environs and his household. His demonstration of control appears innocuous and idyllic as he spends much of his time in a greenhouse, which he built "as a place of controlled ever-flowering life to greet death in" (45).

Into his ritual paradise Valerian had brought with him "some records, garden shears, sixty-four-bulb chandelier, a light blue tennis shirt, and the Principal Beauty of Maine" (9). Valerian married Margaret, twenty years his junior, because, as a seventeen-year-old beauty queen, "she was all red and white," like the candy he manufactured. She is an object of beauty, to be admired and savored, and in the main, her purpose in life for the Street family has been to produce a male heir to the candy kingdom. Margaret functions appropriately; she produces a boy, Michael, and she worships her candy magnate husband, living only "for the concerts Valerian [takes] her to, and dinners for two at restaurants and even alone at home" (49). But as a young woman from modest means, she is completely unprepared for the life of a wealthy wife, and thus she feels "drowned. . . in the spaciousness of the house" and is often left to "amuse herself in solitude" (49), while she alone raises their child.

Their two servants, Sydney and Ondine, also hail from Philadelphia. They have spent their entire adult lives ministering to Valerian's and Margaret's needs, anticipating their every whim, and appearing to be firmly in control of the household's daily affairs. Because of their "industriousness," Sydney and Ondine have assumed the label of "Philadelphia Negroes—the proudest people in the race" (51). They believe themselves superior to lower class blacks but, in reality, because of their accepted positions in the Street conclave, they have only further distanced themselves from any kind of distinct community. They express their class consciousness by never bothering to learn the actual names of the island's black natives and, for instance, call the mansion's gardener Yardman.

Jadine or Jade, orphaned since the age of twelve, is ostensibly spending a few months on the Isle in order to visit her surrogate parents and her benefactors. She is portrayed in the story as the epitome of the "jet-set" character—beautiful, intelligent, refined, and ambitious. With Valerian's assistance, she has completed a degree in Art History, has become a promising Paris model, and she is considering marriage to a wealthy Parisian. But she appears early in the novel as being apprehensive about her future and uncomfortable with her social and financial success. Like Margaret, Jadine is in the process of assuming the role of object and commodity which makes her feel "lonely and inauthentic" (40).

As the narrator introduces the household characters, it becomes increasingly clear that they all share distinct commonalities. Each appears isolated not only from others or from a secure place, but they also appear disconnected from a particular tradition or set of shared values. To compensate for their lack, each character, willingly or not, assumes a position which serves to mask and ultimately evade any signs of difference that may encroach upon them.

On the island, Valerian has established a new beginning for himself. Although he outwardly tells the others that they will someday return to Philadelphia, he never intends to do so.

His uncorrupted greenhouse allows no past and no future; here is the timelessness of a prelapsarian state. It shuts out the inexplicable and allows in only the predictable; and like his study back in Philadelphia, it embodies Valerian's life-long desire to remain aloof and innocent of anything which he can neither understand nor accept. His creed is, as he says: "'I can't be responsible for things outside of my control'" (60). He leads, therefore, an idealistic life of subjective control, full of selectivity and/or denial or experience and free from contradiction and incongruity. In short, the master of the household has safely shaped his perspective into a compartmentalized, self-assertive design.

Margaret is easily inculcated into Valerian's putative design. "This beautiful woman born to two ordinary-looking people . . . who had looked at their beautiful redheaded child with shock and amazement" (96) has been from birth an object of awe and desire. As the narrator explains, because of Margaret's beautiful difference, she experiences a life-long separation from the rest of her family; she is so physically perfect that her parents decide to "step back and let her be" (47). Images of elevation depict the progression that her separation and objectification take; she lives her life on the "two concrete steps" of the family's trailer home, on the "thirty-seven steps at the stadium" where she is crowned, and on the "million wide steps" of Valerian's Philadelphia home (48). Left elevated and isolated, Margaret appears as little more than a projection. Unlike Sula or Pilate, Margaret's difference actually denies the potential for freedom because it has long been culturally institutionalized, frozen in place as it were. Instead, her difference obscures her social and emotional vulnerabilities and leaves her exiled from an empathic human community.

Sydney and Ondine also appear as exiles of another sort. It is apparent later in the novel that the couple typifies a traditional view. Ondine reminds and admonishes Jadine that "'a daughter is a woman that cares about where she come from and takes of them that took care of her'" (242). And Sydney offers his own resigned outlook that "'old black people must be a worrisome thing to the young ones these days'" (244). But

while both servants bemoan the absence of generational continuity, early images of them circumvent their conscious decla-
rations. Both Sydney and Ondine have lived their lives in a
carefully controlled, bourgeois fashion. Their daily lives shut
out difference; there is no funkiness; the narrator presents no
images of deep sensual or emotional eruptions of the kind that
surround Pilate Dead and Eva Peace.

Whatever cultural traditions Sydney and Ondine may share
are seldom made distinct save for their aspirations to
"industriousness" as "Philadelphia Negroes." Their personal
histories, like Valerian's, are held separate and made elusive
by dreams. Valerian, as he watches his plants grow and listens
to music in his greenhouse, often slips into recollective
daydream, but these moments never consciously effect the
direction of his present retirement. Sydney, too, has frequent
nighttime dreams of his childhood in Baltimore. The narrator
says that they are "vivid dreams" (51), yet when he awakens,
he fails to ever recollect them. In short, his dreams of a past,
of a cultural tradition have been displaced in his desire for
assimilation into Valerian's static, well-ordered world.

Images of cultural differences are also revealed to Jadine in
waking vision and dream. But for her, these images trigger a
conscious sense of lack that underscores Jadine's ambivalence
toward black womanhood. Before coming to the Isle, Jadine
experiences her first "vision" at a Paris grocery store as Morrison connects Jadine with her earth mother archetype. She is
struck by the appearance of a "tar-like" African woman whom
the narrator characterizes as a "transcendent beauty . . . that
woman's woman — that mother/sister/she; . . . an unpho-
tographable beauty. . ." (39). "Under her long canary yellow
dress Jadine [knows] there [is] too much hip, too much bust,"
yet she is transfixed by the woman who merely comes to the
store to buy three eggs.

The woman's presence suggests fertility and abundance and
these projections are what make Jadine feel "lonely and
inauthentic." She sees "something in her eyes so powerful"
(38), that she follows the woman outside the store. And as a
symbolic repudiation of Jadine's elevated lifestyle, the African
earth mother "look[s] right at her" (39) and spits on the pave-

ment. Jadine does not clearly understand "why the woman's insulting gesture [has] derailed her," but it nurtures her desire to resist any identification with the woman's maternal difference and, therefore, with her traditional cultural role. She later tells her aunt, "'There are other ways to be a woman, Nanadine'" (243); and for the remainder of the novel, Jade attempts to break free from that part of her which is also "tar-like," as she thinks: "I hate ear hoops, that I don't have to straighten my hair, that Mingus puts me to sleep, that sometimes I want to get out of my skin and be only the person inside — not American — not black — just me" (40).

L'Arbe de la Croix serves as the site of repression, and as such, each character remains safely cloistered in the Isle's controlled freedom from difference and thus in its denial of lack. The household members appear to luxuriate materially and psychologically in their illusory peace, but in order to do so, they assume inarticulate, unempathic, or inaccessible positions. Individual experience unshared dominates the household scenes. Valerian, when not enclosed in the silence of his greenhouse, speaks condescendingly to Margaret and often appears not to understand her thoughts or wishes. Margaret is alone in her hope that her now adult child will visit for Christmas. Sydney and Ondine offer variant views on their masters. He defends Valerian's isolated mode of retirement. Ondine calls Margaret "'the main bitch of the prince'" (29). And although Sydney and Ondine are proud of their niece, both servants tend only to speculate about Jadine's motivations or intentions, and seldom communicate with her directly.

Jadine seems the most detached from the others. Her most engaging encounter in the household comes with her fur-skin coat. She lolls naked upon "the skins of ninety baby seals," and lets her body caress "its dark luxury" (77). From the reader's standpoint, the scene casts an unsympathetic light on Jadine as she uses her coat of dead babies for erotic stimulation. Not only in the juxtaposition of a nude Jadine with a fur coat does the scene reinforce her detachment and objectification, but it also suggests a symbolic imperviousness to her maternal "Other."

With each character dreaming separate, inaccessible dreams, and each character detached physically and psychologically from one another, there exist no connections to the past, no clearly shared values, no collective experience. And as each character remains suspended in their individual assertions and experience, another character surfaces to append his own dream to the island paradise. A few days before Christmas and prior to Michael's expected visit, Margaret is shocked to discover a bedraggled black man hiding in her clothes closet. Sydney escorts the stowaway down to the dining room where Valerian, Margaret, and Jadine had earlier eaten dinner.

Into this carefully controlled cabbage patch comes William Green Smith, nicknamed Son. He is a man with many different names and social security numbers; he is a drifter, a "running man" who exhibits "an inability to stay anywhere for long" (143). Born and raised in Eloe, an all-black Florida village, he is currently on the run for accidentally killing his unfaithful wife. Thus, he too is an exile and has also remained secluded in the house, hiding in pantries and closets during the day, and, at night, spying on the sleeping Jadine whom he falls in love with, "his appetite for her so gargantuan, it [loses] focus and spread[s] to his eyes, the curtains, the moonlight" (119).

As the novel proceeds, Son plainly becomes associated with the many folktales and the folktale archetype of Brer Rabbit, the trickster figure who, in the popular version of the tale, looks to outwit a farmer by first attempting to steal the farmer's intentionally-placed tar baby doll. After Brer Rabbit becomes hopelessly stuck to the doll, he cunningly (and often successfully) pleads for his life. The tales were, of course, symbolic of the master/slave relationship and were intended to train young blacks to cope with bondage by using tactics that could both undermine and outwit the white master. In turn, the tales helped slaves to retain some sense of hope in the face of insuperable odds. In Morrison's version of the tale and for the majority of the novel, Son also hopes to usurp Valerian's representative authority by liberating Jadine from what Son perceives are the false bonding and her appropriated values of the dominant culture.

But Morrison identifies Son's immediate and equally important symbolic relevance in the first pages of *Tar Baby*. At first,
as an unidentified character, Son's initial appearance on the
island is accomplished when he jumps a freighter, swims the
harbor to the Streets' yacht, and hides on the boat as it returns
to Isle des Chevaliers.   While in the process of swimming,
Morrison engulfs Son in maternal imagery.   The sea itself is
made analogous to "the hand of an insistent woman [as] it
push[es] him," and as a "water-lady cupp[ing] him in the palm
of her hand." And as Son struggles to overcome the current,
he emerges as if newly born: ". . . he tore open the water in
front of him, he felt a gentle but firm pressure along his chest,
stomach, and down his thighs" (2).

Son undergoes a rite of passage as he finally submits to the
"water-lady" and decides "to let it carry him for a while" (2).
Once he submits, the "insistent woman" becomes kind, nudg-
ing him and guiding him to the yacht. From the beginning,
Son appears in harmony with this primal mother personified;
and thus, like the African woman, he is positively aligned with
difference and change. On land, he carries with him these as-
sociations as he emerges with "the smell of human afterbirth"
(90) and "the immediate plans of a newborn baby" (119).

Later on, we learn that before his discovery, he has been
kept alive by Thérèse, Ondine's kitchen helper. Thérèse first
appears as a minor character who, like Yardman, is indifferently called Mary by the household. To them, she is less than
significant, but she is actually the first to detect Son's presence
on the island, "for she had seen evidence of the man who ate
chocolate" (89).   Thereafter, she supplies the mystery figure
with an inexhaustible supply of chocolate, invents his identity
by thinking of him as one of the island's blind horsemen, and
she identifies herself as antithetical to Jadine's lifestyle and her
appropriated values by alluding to her as "'The chippy. The
fast-ass'" (92) and as "'the copper Venus'" (98). Thus, even
before she becomes acquainted with Son, she appears to have
assumed the water-lady's role as son's maternal sponsor. And
as the novel progresses, her stature will grow as she becomes
more closely aligned with Son.

To the shock and dismay of Margaret, Ondine, Sydney, and Jade, Valerian invites this part mythic/part realistic man to dinner and welcomes him as a guest in his home. At this point in the text, Valerian appears to act on a whim, and thus, in the absence of his or a narrator's voice, we understand the situation only through the eyes of the other inhabitants of the house. They initially react with horror and disbelief to Son's symbolically timed appearance.   Margaret's discovery of another "son" disrupts her continued expectation of Michael and compels her to seclude herself in Jade's bedroom. She and Jade now share a clear bond of vulnerability in a room of their own.   Son "frightens and disorients" Ondine who believes that "the man upstairs [isn't] a Negro—meaning one of them" (87). Sydney thinks of Son as a "'stinking ignorant swamp nigger . . . a wild-eyed pervert'" (85-6). Both of them remain thoroughly nonplussed by Valerian's acceptance of Son and view the entire situation in an immediately pragmatic way. After all, as Sydney tells Ondine, "'[Son] could have knocked on the back door and got something to eat. Nobody comes in a house and hides in it for days, weeks. . .'" (84).

Jadine perceives Son as "a nasty motherfucker. . . stink nasty . . . like an animal" (105). And like her relations, she also feels dismay in Valerian and wonders if he "know[s] the difference between one Black and another" (107). But in her own recognition and fear of Son's difference, she feels "something more like shame" (105), which creates in her a genuine sense of displacement, as she thinks: "With him she was in strange waters. She had not seen a Black like him in ten years" (108). While she consciously fears and tries to deny Son's difference, her vulnerable sense of lack allows her to identify mountains and savannahs in the "space around his eyes" (68), and to see an earthy, spontaneous presence in his smile which, as the narrator says, "bring[s] once more into view the small dark dogs galloping on silver feet" (97). Like the African woman, Son strikes a primal chord in Jade which has at its center a maternal appeal that becomes for her the site for both attraction and repulsion.

Orphaned, elevated, and vulnerable, Jadine becomes an ideal candidate for what Son wished to impart to her when he had watched her sleep:

> . . . he had thought hard during those times in order to manipulate her dreams, to insert his own dreams into her so she would . . . dream steadily the dreams he wanted her to have about yellow houses with white doors which women opened and shouted Come on in, you honey you! and the fat black ladies in white dresses minding the pie table in the basement of the church and white wet sheets flapping on a line, and the sound of a six-string guitar plucked after supper while children scooped walnuts up off the ground and handed them to her. (102)

Son's dream encompasses the ideal of a rural folk consciousness that emphasizes the importance of origins and nourishment within a stable community. But when Son meets with Jadine, his dream becomes tentative, his hope for its impression is subdued by Jade's own elevated difference:

> But now she was not sleeping; now she was awake and even though she was being still he knew that at any moment she might talk back or, worse, press her dreams of gold and cloisonne and honey-colored silk into him and then who would mind the pie table in the basement of the church? (102-3)

In the first half of the novel, the dreams, images, and portrayals of difference and of lack underline the antithetical development in *Tar Baby*. Some critics take issue with this development; they argue that the household's status quo and their appropriated status quo in opposition to Son's, Thérèse's, and the African woman's primal Otherness is an incompatible, stereotypical, and an entirely reductive model. Darwin T. Turner argues, for example, that the novel's characters ". . . seem too ordinary, too stereotypical—created solely to demonstrate the clash of class and culture" (369). Brina Caplan concludes that ". . . the primary function of Morrison's characters is to voice representative opinions, they arrive on stage vocal and highly conscious, their histories symbolically indicated or merely sketched" (534). And finally, Winfrid Sheed argues that the novel is too obviously contrived, and for the purpose of argument, his point appears here in its entirety:

We have been set up—oh, how we have been set up—for the next act. The folks who live on the hill commonly need these sustaining lies, which everyone is too polite to shoot down. High time now for some *deus ex machina* who will force the truth into the open—at which point the folks will fall apart and/or regroup and go on as if nothing had happened. (119)

Each of these critics present a collectively engaging argument in so much as the first half of the novel may indeed appear too reductive in the development of its character representations; perhaps Morrison has overstated and overdistinguished class and cultural differences to the degree that the novel is reduced to merely valid and invalid positions; and at this point in the text, it appears that Son is, as a savior, reborn into this fallen paradise in order to supplant a distorted, individuated dream with his own dream of a past communality.

However, this collective interpretation fails to locate a significant point of departure in the text whereby Morrison begins to disrupt and eventually collapse the novel's antithetical distinctions. That point begins in Valerian's perceived contradiction in the household's initial response to Son. When Son is escorted by gunpoint to the dining room, Valerian sees "his entire household standing there . . . , all together triumphant, and all together anticipating his command . . . to call the harbor police." But Valerian resists such action because he is particularly struck by the attitude of Jade and her relations toward "a black man who was one of their own." "With faces as black as [Son's], but smug," Valerian surmises that they have appropriated a "bourgeois manner," which is especially galling to him since they are "defending property and personnel that [does] not belong to them. . ." (124).

Of course, from his dominant perspective, Valerian fails to see his recognition as hypocritical; nor is he able to acknowledge that economic class prejudice is inherent in any capitalist system in which all races and classes must necessarily participate. Instead, Valerian revels in his perceived contradiction; he enjoys "the dismay that his invitation [has] thrown them into" (125), because, by keeping his subjects uncertain and insecure, it solidifies his isolated, dictatorial position. But more importantly, his invitation opens out in the text a black cultural condition that humanist literary critics choose to ignore.

Humanist discourse strives to identify antipodal situations in order to arrive at thematically unifying solutions. The categories in *Tar Baby* are endlessly apparent: rich/poor, privileged/downtrodden, natural/unnatural, bourgeois/folk, freedom/isolation, stasis/movement, authentic/inauthentic, etc. If, as humanist readers, we remain tied to oppositional perspectives, we assume, like Valerian, the other's gaze, reveling in the apparent contradiction because we can manage it through valorization and derision. But for the remainder of the novel, Morrison deconstructs binary opposition in order to demonstrate that, for blacks or for any minority, no position can be made mutually exclusive; under the gaze of the dominant group, all positions in black consciousness tenuously converge at mutual attraction and repulsion; neither individual assertion nor collective tradition remain fixed, rarefied positions. Therefore, the novel's black characters demonstrate not so much a "clash of class and culture," but a condition of marginality, a cultural given in black life that is infused with desire and repression, with acceptance and withdrawal.

Morrison centers this cultural duplicity in the burgeoning love affair between Jade and Son. Both express a desire and repulsion toward the other that immediately manifests itself in their first encounter. When Son enters unannounced into Jade's bedroom, she is at once transfixed by his image that she envisions in the mirror. As she stares into the mirror, she perceives his "wild, aggressive, vicious hair" while she struggles "to pull herself away from his image . . . and to yank her tongue from the roof of her mouth." To free herself "at last from the image" which, to her, "look[s] physically overpowering," she frames it into "the picture that only Margaret had seen clearly" in her bedroom. Once she is "freed at last," she turns to the real presence of Son in her bedroom, but sees only "the riverbed darkness of his face" (97).

In this scene, Jadine's impulsions undulate through a series of dyadic unifications. Attraction and repulsion, eruption and repression, stabilization and closure all merge into her mirrored creation. She finds it difficult to free herself from the image because its eruption reflects her desire for that "wild, aggressive, vicious" difference which she has repressed and which she now consciously projects upon Son's appearance. Like small dogs and large spaces, from the interstices of Jade's consciousness emanate a nebulous, imaged self that perpetuates her attraction to that which she is not.

Implicit in Jadine's projections is the Sula-like desire to enter into a more fluid, more sensual zone, but she is equally repulsed by these discontinuous zones of desire because in them she locates the cultural ambivalences in her life. Conditioned to seek the security of a singular, controlling position, Jadine frames or, in effect, freezes Son's mirrored image in the same way she assumes that Margaret would. In Margaret, Son's image of difference inspires fear and hatred, and thus, in aligning herself again with the dominant other, Jade disavows her imaged self and believes she can return to the safety of her acculturated self-conceptions.

From the beginning, Jadine has located both positive and negative characteristics in Son; obviously, then, Jade's momentary attempt at closure can never fully resolve her undulations of attraction and repulsion so long as Son's destabilizing presence remains to inspire reflection. What becomes even more significant in the bedroom scene, then, is that as she looks the into indeterminate "riverbed darkness" of Son's face, she and we begin to locate the real presence of Son and, in doing so, the underlying paradigm of a positive/negative evaluation within the text continues to collapse. Previously enveloped in and associated with myth and imagery, Morrison begins to open out Son's character as he assumes more human proportions and exposes the nature of his own cultural duplicity. A humanist reading may posit that Jade represents false bonding and false values while Son represents true bonding and true values; he is, in short, a reminder to Jade of a heritage that she attempts to deny. And clearly there is divergence in the two characters; Jadine, the acculturated orphan, is presented as a character who lacks connection while

Son seems to symbolize a wild zone of the natural and sensual that encompasses rural landscapes and communal traditions.

But one cannot ignore the fissure that remains in this closed reading. Appearing as a kind of community outlaw, Son seems to represent ancient properties of his community and, therefore, he appears dedicated to the articulation, dissemination, and thereby the upholding of its communal spirit. So much so that there is almost a religious fervor associated with Son's narrative; his voice overwhelms us with his definitive pronouncements; like a righteous preacher he tells Jade: "'Anybody ask you where you from, you give them five towns. You're not from anywhere. I'm from Eloe'" (229). So overwhelming is his voice throughout the text that he may appear as a unitary self; on his side are connection, passion, a sense of values and commitment, all of which can be easily appropriated and therefore valorized by readers.

But there is much that Morrison leaves us to explore in Son's character. Lingering just beneath Son's stabilizing enunciations lies his most obviously contradictory position of community outlaw and, deeper still, the destabilizing desire in his attraction to Jade. Nothing could be more clearly oxymoronic than Son as the community outlaw; the label itself suggests connection and disconnection, commitment and noncommitment. Yet because of his strindent, confident voice professing culture and communal values, we may forget that his status as outlaw signifies, among many things, distance, disconnection, isolation; and unlike Pilate, Son carries with him to the island no accoutrements or demonstrable skills and/or practices associated with culture or community. Admittedly, he is out of his element, but he nonetheless appears most personally detached from culture and community, shorn of all but his convictioned voice exiled among his new-found exiled group.

The "not" in Son is also a sign of deceptive multiplicity because, as he enmeshes himself in the island household, he becomes all things to all people. To Valerian, Son is a practical and comfortable presence; with mirrors, he drives the ants from the greenhouse, he shakes flowers into full bloom, and he tells Valerian a joke about "'the three colored whores who went to heaven'" (127). Toward Ondine and Sydney, he is penitential; he comes to them with respect and shows remorse for his irregular behavior. The two servants are pleased by his "quiet and respectful" (141) nature. With Thérèse and Yardman (whose true name Son learns is Gideon), he appears more "himself," as the narrator tells us, "he stretch[es] his legs and permit[s] himself a hearthside feeling, comfortable and free of posture and phony accents" (129). But even in the island natives' satisfying presence, he feels a certain discomforting desire for the Otherness of Jade; he doesn't "want her in Gideon's mind, his eye. It unnerve[s] him to think that Gideon [has] looked at her at all" (133).

While Son appears confidently son-like to the others, dutiful and congenial, his pose lacks the same invincibility around Jade; her very presence destabilizes his carefully managed poses and instills in him a genuine sense of uncertainty; he thinks that "he want[s] to go home but that woman [is] on his mind" (144). When he first speaks to her, he is insulting and sarcastic. He accuses Jade of being and acting like a "white girl" (103); and upon learning that she is a model, Son lewdly suggests that her career is beholden to a kind of "casting-couch" mentality. Yet his overt repulsion to Jade's difference wavers in his realization that his insults merely "keep her unhinging beauty from afflicting him and keeping him away from home" (144).

Jade's conscious response to Son also contributes to his destabilization. She resists his dreams and insults because, as she thinks, she is determined "never to be broken in the hands of any man" (106). Thus, in spite of her fear and desire, she assumes control and is prepared to repulse Son with her own forms of belittlement. In their second solitary encounter, Son asks Jade to lunch on the beach, and in their conversations, Son tells some of his life story. To Jade's cosmopolitan sensibilities, Son's dream for "'something nice and simple and personal'" sounds mundane and "lazy" (146). She calls him "'a big country baby'" (147) who, while being worldy-wise, lacks a completeness of character. Without fully realizing it, Jade locates the basis for Son's multiplicity; despite his overt solidarity with self and place, he projects a vulnerability that sometimes manifests itself in deceptive poses and, at other times, finds expression in his visionary attraction to Jade.

Son is clearly enamored of Jade; like the alluring tar baby, Jade's antithetical position appeals to Son; he is curious about and impressed with her work, her life-style, her intellectual and practical knowledge. As a community outlaw, Son, according to Dorothy H. Lee, "seeks to recapture lost security, nurturing, and fraternity . . . but also . . . he has encountered a jewel he wants to possess" and to take home to the brier patch of Eloe. Here the analogy to the tar baby folktale itself begins to collapse when Son's behavior transcends the manipulative principle of the folktale. Lee goes on to valorize Son by again claiming that Jade "entraps the intruding disturber of the status quo" (355). But the entrapment more fully resides in Son's own desire for and possession of Jade. Demonstrating his inner-directed desire, Son begs her to understand and accept him: "'I'm not crazy, Jadine. Raw, maybe, but not nuts'" (153). And he wishes to touch her feet in order to remove the disgust she feels for him and to achieve a coherent bond with her saying, "'I don't have a real life like most people, I've missed a lot'" (152).

Where Jade has been and what she has become, her difference, which Son is so paradoxically ignorant of, repulsed by, and yet intrigued with, provides him with a sense of purpose, a vision of "a real life." To return to Eloe with his "high yaller" beauty would be Son's ultimate achievement of the phallic imperative. He would find self-worth in the possession and subservience of an unusually prized object. He would appropriate difference in order to shore up his own vulnerable sense of lack and, like a Macon Dead, he would then stabilize his attraction and repulsion by securing an ideally singular, dominant position.

But the necessary condition of being an exile dictates that Son waver between attraction and repulsion; the "disturber" is himself disturbed by difference and lack; he is attracted to and dreams of possessing the Otherness that Jade projects, yet at the same time he overtly condemns it and is repulsed by it. Inversely, Jadine is attracted to Son's cultural difference, yet she is ashamed and fearful of it. Both desire but do not desire what each lacks; and thus, what unfolds in the text is not a simple oppositional, positive/negative paradigm, but Morrison's complex depiction of two black characters split internally and externally by multiple and conflicting roles, expectations, and desires.

For the remainder of the novel, Jadine and Son attempt to resolve their mutually conflicting and intersectional positions. To do so, they must necessarily continue to negotiate between attraction and repulsion, between difference and lack which, as the narrative proceeds, is further underscored by Jade's and Son's perceptive distinctions between the actual and the dream, between the real and the ideal. The couple's first experiential attempts to resolve their perceptive difference and lack is propelled and preceded by a serious form of rupture within the island household. As the houshold mediates between apprehension and acceptance of Son, his disruptive difference, little by little, exposes an unspoken narrative that forms a subtext in the novel, and culminates in the exposure of Margaret's maternal secret—that she habitually abused Michael when he was a baby. Seemingly incidental to the valent relationship of Jade and Son, Morrison has been building a second suspense.

Michael's presence looms throughout the first half of the story; much talk among the household surrounds his impending visit, and yet he never appears at Christmas time. There are a number of disturbing signs that, in retrospect, collectively serve to unmask the mystery of his absence from the household. Valerian laments to Jadine of his estrangement from Michael, and he blames Margaret because, as he says, "'She made him think poetry was incompatible with property. She made a perpetual loser of one of the most beautiful, the brightest boy in the land'" (63).

But Valerian's estrangement runs much deeper. Since the narrator offers no detailed perspective, no revelations about Valerian's relationship with his son, and since Valerian's own disengaged narrative underlines his peripheral nurturing role, his interaction and influence in his son's life has been minimal at best; he indicts himself for his lack of loving involvement and meaningful intervention in family matters which is, in the patriarchal order, what he has been conditioned to do.   His reaction to his conditional disengagement is to hyper-withdraw into his greenhouse which itself is an actual symbol for his self-induced estrangement; he builds it, as the narrator says, when he comes to know that Michael will forever "be a stranger to him" (45).   For Michael, then, the greenhouse is not a site of welcome and hospitality.

Another clue to Michael's permanent un-presence on the island is Ondine's vitriolic hatred for the "Principal Beauty." Ondine tells her husband that Michael doesn't wish to be near his mother because she is "'not natural'" (30). At this point we might assume that Ondine's anger stems from Margaret's desire to cook the Christmas dinner.   Certainly Ondine's anger toward Margaret's intrusion in what the servant perceives as her kitchen is understandable, but Ondine's anger is much too vituperative and deep-seated to be merely the result of momentary grumpiness.   She is distraught by the very idea that Margaret and Michael could be together especially when, as she tells Sydney, "'. . . he don't want to be nowhere near her. And I can't say as I blame him, mother though she be'" (29).

Early in the novel, it becomes apparent that the entire household is reacting to an unspoken conflict, and the mystery deepens and yet assumes a sharper focus when Valerian reveals to Jade his most endearing image of Michael as a child. He tells Jade that he had frequently found Michael under a bathroom sink, singing and humming a "'lovely song,' 'looking in the dark for something soft.'" Valerian had made no attempt to discover exactly why Michael would hide under the sink.   His conditioned disengagement causes him to base his understanding only on conjecture; he believed, at the time, as he tells Jade, that he "'sometimes had a feeling that [Margaret] didn't talk to him very much. . . .'" As an observer, Valerian only witnesses the relationship between mother and son, and he perceives that Margaret's behavior is "'hot and cold'" toward her son, while Michael "'seemed to miss her so, need her so that when she was attentive he was like a slave to her'" (64).

Taken collectively, Morrison tosses off all of these disturbing signs seemingly without connection or development. Only in re-reading can we begin to link together these mysterious clues. For instance, while Son's presence in the bedroom closet frightens Margaret into hiding, Valerian accepts him like a friend and a son because Son is a connective catalyst for Valerian's memory of his failure to reach out to his true hiding son. Shortly after Son is discovered, Valerian imagines that he had seen "his only living son in the dining room [which was] probably the consequence of describing the sink business to Jade." Valerian believes that "Michael seemed to be smiling at him last night . . . and that was part of the reason he invited the black man to have a seat, the forepresence of Michael in the dining room" (123). Momentarily, at least, Valerian, in his own illusory and pathetic way, succeeds through Son in closing the distance between himself and Michael.

Son is also a catalyst in another way; his disruptive, rebellious presence compels Ondine to expose Margaret's secret to the entire household. Ondine learns that, without consulting her, Valerian has fired her kitchen help, Gideon and Thérèse, for stealing apples. His act sends a message to both Ondine and Sydney that they are merely servants, that their opinions about household affairs are not valued, and that their bourgeois illusions have accorded them little or no respect. In short, Ondine recognizes her own difference that she and Sydney had masked beneath bourgeois values and ideals.

Valerian is astonished that anyone would question his imperial control: "'It's not all right,' he tells Margaret, 'Whose house is this?'" But Son asserts that "'two people are going to starve so your wife [can] play American mama and fool around in the kitchen'" (177); his defiance bolsters Ondine's own sense of outrage toward Valerian's insensitivity. She rends the innocent, illusory veil that Valerian has maintained in the emblematic distance of his greenhouse by exposing Margaret's violation of maternal responsibility:

"You cut him up. You cut your baby up. Made him bleed for you. For fun you did it. Made him scream, you, you freak. You crazy white freak. She did, Ondine addressed the others, still shouting. She stuck pins in his behind. Burned him with cigarettes. Yes, she did, I saw her; I saw his little behind. She burned him!" (179)

In Ondine's revelation, Valerian is forced to acknowledge that his ignorant and therefore innocent position is actually a subterfuge for the guilt he feels for his inaction: "He had not known because he had not taken the trouble to know. He was satisfied with what he did know. Knowing more was inconvenient and frightening" (209).   By contrast, Ondine's knowledge makes her unwillingly complicit in Margaret's unfathomable acts of abuse, and her silence also allows Margaret to continue, as she later tells Margaret: "'There was nobody to tell. It was woman stuff. . . . If I told Sydney he might tell Mr. Street and then we'd be out of a job. . .'" (207). But to her credit, Ondine had done what Valerian was incapable of doing; she gives love and consolation to the abused child: "'I used to hold him and pet him. He was so scared'" (179).

After the collapse of his illusion, Valerian begins "going back to his greenhouse," but it is no longer "a place of controlled ever-flowering life"; he allows it to return to its natural cycle of growth and decay. The narrator tells us that he "didn't sow or clip or transpose. Things grew or died where and how they pleased. Isle des Chevaliers filled in the spaces that had been the island's to begin with" (208). Margaret attempts to share her burden with her devastated husband. She is released from her preoccupation with Michael's return by Valerian's regression into a kind of infancy. She benignly mothers him and the transmission of her story of failed nurturance is made analogous to maternal feeding: "Margaret told her husband in pieces. Little by little, she spooned it out to him a sip here a drop there" (203).

But it is too late to remake Valerian; he wants to "go to Michael. Find him, touch him, rub him, hold him in his arms . . . but [his] spastic legs [defy] him" (200). In his innocent isolation, he realizes that, about his wife and son, "he knew nothing . . . and there was something so foul in that, something in the crime of innocence so revolting it paralyzed him." He believes now that he and his orderly life are shattered beyond repair:

> He was guilty, therefore, of innocence. Was there anything so loath-some as a willfully innocent man? Hardly. An innocent man is a sin before God. Inhuman and therefore unworthy. No man should live without absorbing the sins of his kind, the foul air of his innocence, even if it did wilt rows of angel trumpets and cause them to fall from their vines. (209)

Like the Hawthornian character who fatefully suffers forever for the sin of disconnection from humanity, Valerian is ironically left with the peril of a second, guilt-ridden childhood. But in it, he belatedly comes to accept that vulnerability must be a necessary part of the human condition, and thus while he has remained willfully innocent, "Margaret knew the bottomlessness—she had looked at it, dived in it and pulled herself out—obviously tougher than he" (209).

And indeed, it is Margaret who manages afterwards to hold together "the demoralized house" (187). She cannot hope to explain her unacceptable acts of abuse beyond her own sense of inadequacy that "when [Michael] was an infant he seemed to want everything of her, and she didn't know what to give" (50). But she nonetheless appears to Valerian as strengthened from the experience precisely because she has long accepted her action, however deplorable or inexplicable, as one of life's painful possibilities. She tells Valerian, "'I have done it, lived with it,'" and unlike Valerian who is "wasting away" (204) from his exposure to experience, Margaret remains a survivor who has, in her own way, retained a multiple perspective. In the end, Margaret continues to console Valerian, assuring him that Michael still loves them; she assures Ondine and Sydney that she will not dismiss them from the household; and further, she asks for and receives Ondine's grudging forgiveness while telling her that "'we're both childless now, Ondine. And we're both stuck here. We should be friends. It's not too late'" (208).

It is important to note, however, that the aforementioned developments are withheld from the reader. Following Ondine's revelation, we see only a "demoralized house" that is momentarily shocked into silence. Thereafter, the focus in the text quickly returns to Son and, most importantly, to Jadine. While Son is the catalyst for rupture, the problematic nexus of maternity and nurturance once again makes Jadine the novel's center of reaction and resistance. In the similar way that she fled from the "authentic," maternal presence of the African woman, Jadine flees from a distorted vision of mothering gone awry. On this occasion, however, Margaret's negative vision does not make Jadine feel lonely or inauthentic; instead it invigorates her because it confirms her suspicions about that which she is not—or should become. And with Son's acquiescence, it also provides Jade with the opportunity to create her own alternative social model.

In New York City, the place she feels most at home, Jade envisions that she and Son will lead a fairytale existence as metropolitan bons vivants. She thinks of her home "with an orphan's delight" which, while it suggests her childlike pleasure in the city's unpredictability, it also foretells the ephemeral quality of such pleasure. Here in New York is a kind of attraction and repulsion that seems more categorical and more stable. Jadine sees the city as a black woman's town where the manifesto is "Talk Shit, Take None" (191). Here is a place for self-confidence and self-assertion where a past of traditional roles and ways does not intrude, nor is it perceived as desirable, and any reminder of cultural alienation or exile are suspended by a flurry of the homogenized and consumerized now.

Son sees none of his nurturing desire for home and fraternity in Jadine's social model. He assumes a darker, grimmer perspective of the city, and within his gaze is located a historical aperçu of African-American social, geographical, and cultural disruption and transformation. He even wonders if he has been transported from the past and is now "being confronted with a whole new race of people. . ." (187). "Where [are] the Thérèses and Gideons of New York?" (186), Son wonders. In this urban setting, Son finds no traces of identity or place; he encounters a setting that he perceives as fabricated and prefabricated. He sees it as a place where "the street [is] choked with beautiful males who had found the whole business of being black and men at the same time too difficult and so they'd dumped it." On television, he sees "black people in whiteface playing black people in blackface," and in the "televised laughter" there remains no trace of "irony or defiance or genuine amusement. Now all he hears [are] shrieks of satisfaction" (186).

But Son does not respond to his perceptions of absence with his usual hatred or rebellion because "here pre-stressed concrete and steel contained anger, folded it back on itself to become a craving for things rather than vengeance. Still, he thought of it not just as love, but as rescue" (190). While the poles of attraction and repulsion appear to give way to a loving, natural bond between Son and Jadine, Son has placed a condition on their love. He has agreed to come to New York to assuage Jadine's delight with the calculated hope that he may rescue her from her own vision of happiness. So his repulsion remains, but subdued by attraction and managed with loving deception ". . . to keep the climate mild for her, to hold back his hands if need be thunder. . ." (189), and thus to carefully persuade her that his vision of Eloe is correct.

Throughout their time in New York, then, and in spite of the apparent bliss and harmony that the two lovers share there, Son "insists" on returning to Eloe. And Jadine is persuaded because she, in her growing "devotion" to Son (192), is becoming increasingly repulsed by her own perceptions of fabrication:

> She listened to him and nodded, thinking anywhere with him would be all right. She was completely happy. After all those sexually efficient men, all those foreplay experts and acrobats, and nonverbal equipment men, his wildness and fumbling, his corny unself-conscious joy was like blue-sky water. (193-4)

Jadine assumes a typically naive, modern-day attraction to that which may provide an authenticating pose. We seek in others and aspire, within ourselves, to the spontaneous, the adventuresomeness, the natural, the free-spirited otherness proferred by commercial media; and like Jadine, we buy into a devotional need for what the narrator tells us Jadine finally achieves—"a brand-new childhood" (197) that promises a brand-new life while denying all forms of socio-historical conditioning.

Of course their affair does contain genuine elements of a mature, loving relationship. The two appear to need each other, they sustain and play off each other. With Jadine, Son has "a future. A reason for hauling ass in the morning. No more moment to moment play-it-as-it-comes existence" (188). Essentially a lonely man and tired of being a running man, Son believes that Jadine, with her desire for success, improvement, and upward movement, can provide him with a structural existence. But he has also become devoted to her, recognizing her deeper qualities, seeing that "underneath her efficiency and know-it-all sass were wind chimes" (189).

Jadine feels "unorphaned" by Son; he gives her a feeling of security that she has seldom known: "He cherished and safeguarded her. When she woke in the night from an uneasy dream she had only to turn and there was the stability of his shoulder and his limitless, eternal chest." Her own sense of isolation and exile, which has given her the protective coloration of arrogance and aggression, gives way to a softer, more sensitive side of her character. "No part of her was hidden from him"; all that is colorful, sparkling, soothing, and beautiful surfaces in Jadine, and for a short time, in their insulation from the outside world, Jadine and Son are cast as ideal lovers, as the narrator says, "They were the last lovers in New York City—the first in the world—so their passion was inefficient and kept no savings account. They spent it like Texans" (197).

Ultimately, however, Son's ulterior design to rescue Jadine has worked its magic. In their ideal state of apparent harmony and bliss, Jade agrees to visit Eloe and thus presents Son with the potential of inserting her into his bedroom dream-vision of Eloe. In Chapter Nine of the novel, Morrison juxtaposes Son's vision with a close-up, qualified view of Eloe, and in doing so, she demystifies Son's site of spirit and desire within its modern-day context. At first, when the couple nears Eloe and Jadine shouts, "'This is a town?'" (210), we may assume that her reaction is in keeping with her sometimes abrasive and condescending character. But in this chapter, Morrison allows us to see only Jadine's perspective as she and we become acquainted with Eloe; and while her view is skewed by fear and unfamiliarity, there is nonetheless no contrastive voice to counter-balance Jadine's increasingly definitive view.

Jadine immediately feels constricted by the community's gender divisions into rigid male and female roles. She cannot "understand (or accept) her being shunted off with Ellen and the children while the men grouped on the porch and, after a greeting, ignored her" (212). Like Janie Woods in Hurston's *Their Eyes Were Watching God*, Jadine is determined to resist such categorization. In hopes of enlivening her welcome with an apparently harmless act, Jade takes photographs of willing community members. But Son snatches the camera from her and, at the same time, lets it be known to the residents that he and Jade will be sleeping in separate bedrooms. His motion and message have a dual purpose: He seeks accommodation by attempting to expel all images and thus collective thoughts of unnatural behavior that he assumes Jade is projecting. And in his anticipation of community response, Son's action is a signal to Jade to accept a passive role.

His accommodating behavior, however, only exacerbates Jadine's resistance to this provincial community: "Paleolithic, she thought. I am stuck here with a pack of Neanderthals who think sex is dirty or strange or something and he is standing here almost thirty years old doing it too." And while Jade thinks Son "accommodating beyond all belief" (221), he, too, senses that his romantic, dream-vision of Eloe is unraveling. "'One more night, baby'" (220), Son tells Jade as if, in assuring her, he also confirms that the uncomfortable, stagnating reality of Eloe will soon end for both of them.

The Eloe of Son's dream-vision, the "yellow houses with white doors" and "fat black ladies in white dresses minding the pie table" (102) is exposed by Jadine as an image of his desire, a wish fulfillment rooted in private nostalgia, and bearing no resemblance to a real past. We come to see Eloe as a community of tough-minded, pragmatic, and stoic people who do not dream Son's dream of "pie tables" and "six-string guitars." Here are no representations of call and response or scenes of instructive oral folktales; here are no vital or fluid images of a folk tradition. Here is a town so deeply ingrained and isolated in convention that it offers Son and Jade no outlet for desire or fulfillment. In the midst of Son's silent acquiescence, Jadine concludes that "Eloe [is] rotten and more boring than ever. A burnt-out place. . . . [And] all that Southern small-town country romanticism [is] a lie, a joke, kept secret by people who [can] not function elsewhere" (223).

But Jadine's conclusion does not diffuse the oppositional flux that remains in the text. Jadine has a final nightmare vision which convinces her that, for her, in Eloe, there is "maybe a past but definitely no future and finally there [is] no interest" (223). The "night women"—several women from Eloe, Aunt Ondine, and the African woman from Paris—crowd ino Jade's claustrophobic bedroom, and together they seem to Jadine "somehow in agreement with each other about her, and [are] all out to get her, tie her, bind her. Grab the person she has worked hard to become and choke it off with their soft loose tits" (225). Out of fear and guilt, Jade believes that the night women are condemning her for having ignored the traditional, maternal role in favor of material, success-oriented ambitions. She expresses momentary attraction to the image of fertility and nurturance by telling them, "'I have breasts, too. . . .'" But ultimately, she is repulsed when she concludes that they do not believe her as they hold ". . . their own [breasts] higher and push their own further out. . ." (222).

In Morrison's essay, "City Limits, Village Values," she writes that ". . . present in village fiction is the ancestor. The advising, benevolent, protective, wise Black ancestor is imagined as surviving in the village. . ." (39). Thus, while the reality of Eloe denies the Ideal, and the actual demystifies the dream, Morrison, through Jadine's imaginings, perpetuates the "profound values" (43) of the maternal ancestor who, in spite of Eloe's stagnant reality, cannot be erased from imagination and memory. Cultural memory, then, continues to haunt Jadine and will continue to do so until she is able to resolve the cultural disparity between what the maternal ancestor represents and who she has become.

For Son, the choice between acceptance and withdrawal is precluded by his return to the Isle of Chevaliers; he returns to the site of desire and lack, hopelessly entangled in attraction and repulsion, wanting neither to accept nor withdraw:

> And what was he doing thinking that Drake and Soldier and Ernie Paul were more precious than Catherine the Great's earrings or that the pie ladies were in danger unless he alone protected them and kept them alive. So he had changed, given up fraternity, or believed he had, until he saw Alma Estee in a wig the color of dried blood. Her sweet face, her midnight skin mocked and destroyed by the pile of synthetic fried blood on her head. It was all mixed up. But he could have sorted it out if she had just stood there like a bougainvillea in a girdle, like a baby jaguar with lipstick, or, like an avocado with earrings, and let him remove it. (257-8)

The island girl, Alma Estee, stands as the matrix of corruption and despair that culture and tradition undergo in the presence of desire and lack. Repulsed by the image of self, Alma appropriates the attracted presence of the dominant other and creates an image of cultural distortion. But more significantly, Son's reactions to what she signifies are "all mixed up"; he would prefer (desire) the fusion of the natural with the unnatural, the "bougainvillea in a girdle," rather than gaze upon the mutual impurities of past and present, of the Eloe and Jade that he sees in Alma, and that serve only to deflate his oppositional righteousness.

Son seeks closure for his vacillation and determines that freedom from desire and lack can still be found in Jadine. He continues to deny that his dream, his ideal cannot be inserted into or even merged with Jade, and that he no more can survive choosing Jade than he can endure losing her. At this final stage in the novel, Thérèse plays her pivotal maternal role. In Son's state of cultural irresolution, Thérèse directs him through her primal vision which, as a means of closure, can find its expression only in the simplicity and certainty of legend and myth. In the novel's moment of magical transformation, Thérèse guides Son again through the water and presents him with his mythic alternative:

> "The men are waiting for you. You can choose now. You can get free of her. They are waiting in the hills for you. They are naked and they are blind too . . . they race those horses like angels all over the hills where the rain forest is, where the champion daisy trees still grow. Go there. Choose them." (263)

When Son obeys Thérèse and accepts his mythic role as a blind horseman, he is, as his emergence onto the island suggests, reborn and returns to the island as one of her naked sons:

> First he crawled the rocks one by one, one by one, till his hands touched shore and the nursing sound of the sea was behind him. He felt around, crawled off and then stood up. Breathing heavily with his mouth open he took a few tentative steps. (263)

He thereafter assumes the form of the eternal running man as "the mist [lifts] and the trees [step] back a bit as if to make the way easier for a certain kind of man" (263-4). Merging the actual with the dream, and "looking neither to the left nor to the right," Son runs "Lickety-split, Lickety-lickety-lickety-split" (264) into a collective narrative (un)consciousness which, in its communal blindness, depends upon seclusion and invisibility as a means of expressing social difference and freedom.

Jadine, grounded as she is in the real, is accorded no such mythic expulsion in the text. It has been argued, and rightly so, that Jadine's withdrawal from the ancestor and her eventual return to Paris indicates, for instance, as Marilyn E. Mobley suggests, "her refusal to define herself in terms of familial past, historical tradition, and cultural heritage" (767). Jade's withdrawal is precipitated by her own perception that what Son and Eloe offer is ". . . to settle for wifely competence when she could be almighty, to settle for fertility rather than originality, nurturing instead of building" (231). Morrison comments, in an interview with Claudia Tate, that "Black women seem able to combine the nest and the adventure" (124). Thus, judging from the author's extra-textual statements, Jadine's withdrawal from this combination and her acceptance of disconnection from a cultural heritage serve as an indictment against her for denying the cultural knowledge that may further empower her.

Tar Baby appears, then, as a cautionary, instructive tale which, as Mobley points out, ". . . shows that the black woman who denies her historical connections and sacred properties risks psychic chaos and alienation. . ." (770). But given the circumstances surrounding Jadine's choices, it appears more likely that "psychic chaos" and "alienation" are not simply risked, they remain, as they have throughout the novel, as ongoing, fluctuating agents inherent within the text's narrative design. While Jadine appears to choose and, in doing so, rejects cultural memory and imagination, they continue to intrude. As she departs for Paris, she consciously believes that "she [is] the safety she long[s] for"; in her momentary resolve, she expresses, unlike Son or Valerian, a transcendence of place and circumstance as a means of order and identity, and locates it instead within the potentialities of self.

Yet her determination to withdraw from memory and place only slightly conceals her desire for that which she is not. Jadine's fleeing thoughts and final presence in the text are made analogous to the singular industry of soldier ants: "The life of their world requires organizations so tight and sacrifice so complete there is little need for males and they are seldom produced" (250). The queen "seals herself off from all society" (251) in her "shamelessly single-minded" (250) need for order and control; there is "no time for dreaming," no time for fluidity and funk, no eruptions into otherness. Although, as the narrator goes on to say, "she might get wind of a summer storm one day"; she may remember "the rush of wind on her belly — the stretch of fresh wings, the blinding anticipation and herself, there, airborne, suspended, open, trusting, frightened, determined, vulnerable . . . , and she may embrace, "for an entire second" (251), the "summer storm" of a collective identity and place.

Chapter VII

Beloved: The Paradox of a Past and Present Self and Place

Morrison's fifth novel, *Beloved* (1988), opens within the historical present of 1873 and into the home of a former slave, Sethe, and her daughter, Denver. Here, too, is a past of Sethe's two sons, Howard and Bugler, and of a now dead grand matriarch, Baby Suggs. Most of all, there is "the gray and white house on Bluestone Road"; it is "spiteful" and "full of a baby's venom," and has caused Sethe's sons to flee long ago and made "victims" of those left behind. There is a ghost in the house, that much we know; it is a ghost that shatters mirrors, that puts its "tiny hand prints" in the cake, and that leaves "another kettleful of chickpeas smoking in a heap on the floor" (3). Those who remain wage ". . . a perfunctory battle against the outrageous behavior of the place" and yet they tolerate its presence in the hope that "an exchange of views or something [would] help" (4). For twelve years, "no visitors of any sort and certainly no friends" (13) have entered the house on Bluestone Road; here is a primary source of repression and repulsion, of fear and flight, of victims and death; here linear and circular time and space collide so that past and present cohabit and leave us and the house's residents suspended in a fragmented, multi-dimensional reality.

Fragments emerge just enough to expose their repression. Sethe "work[s] hard to remember as close to nothing as [is] safe. Unfortunately her brain [is] devious." And the presence of "the dead one" (6), of a child who as Sethe tells Denver, "'wasn't even two years old when she died,'" presents itself as a reminder to Sethe that, as Baby Suggs knows, "death [is] anything but forgetfulness" (4); it is an imprint upon the soul, and in *Beloved*, it remains at the center of all life and memory. But Sethe "count[s] on the stillness of her own soul" in order to forget "the other one: the soul of her baby girl" (5), and thus she actively denies life and memory in hopes that death will not intrude. Sethe's "serious work" in life is "beating back the past" (173).

But she also knows in her "devious brain" that the past is the source of her present self. The margins of past consciousness continue to collide within the text; form and content merge as Sethe's consciousness expands to include these fragments of a past, of Baby Suggs, as she tells Sethe: "'You lucky. You got three left. Three pulling at your skirts and just one raising hell from the other side. Be thankful, why don't you? I had eight. Every one of them gone away from me'" (5). And then Sethe's consciousness expands further back to the Sweet Home plantation, "rolling, rolling, rolling out before her eyes" (6), welling up into a hopeful living memory. Soon Paul D, one of the men from the old plantation, stands before her in the present. He stands at the apex of memory and life, and signals the beginning of their immergence into death.

It has been eighteen years since she has seen Paul D. He is like a brother or a lover come, he says, to see Baby Suggs (dead now since 1865), but mostly come to see Sethe who smiles and is excited by his living presence of memory: "This is the way they were—had been. All of the Sweet Home men, before and after Halle, treated her to a mild brotherly flirtation, so subtle you had to scratch for it" (7). The two together reveal in memory the fragments of a gentle though ominous personal history. Just beneath a nostalgic landscape of the two selves and their place in memory lies the undertow of death. Paul D sees a young Sethe, "Halle's girl—the one with iron eyes and backbone to match," but just as quickly, he recalls that when "schoolteacher" arrived at Sweet Home, he ". . . broke three more Sweet Home men and punched the glittering iron out of Sethe's eyes, leaving two open wells that did not reflect firelight" (9).

When Paul D enters the house, it exudes a sadness "so thoroughly he want[s] to cry" (9), but he does not. They,

Sethe, Denver, and now Paul D, are joined by and enveloped in this sadness. "'My daughter,' Sethe says, 'The one I sent ahead with boys'" (10) is the sadness that gives the house its character, and supplies them with a living history, personal, private, ignored, shameful. It is a living history of unspoken sorrow, frightening, and familiar to all, the history of a self and place both distorted and revived by individual consciousness—but "'Rebuked,' Denver tells Paul D, 'Lonely and rebuked'" (13). But memory rebuked is not memory concealed. Sethe speaks to Paul D of the sorrow and desire through memory deferred:

> "I got a tree on my back and a haint in my house, and nothing in between but the daughter I am holding in my arms. No more running—from nothing. I will never run from another thing on this earth. I took one journey and I paid for the ticket, but let me tell you something, Paul D Garner: it cost too much! Do you hear me? It cost too much. . . ." (15)

But a tale is to be told, a narrative journey will go forth, and thus this shifting, unfixed textual folksong leaks out with soft, unfocused visions of warm and horrific memory. The memory of a white girl who helps Sethe escape; the memory of white boys who suck milk from her breasts; the memory of "schoolteacher" who, with a cowhide strap, carves out the tree on Sethe's back which, as she says, "'. . . grows there still'" (17). All deferred, yet erupting in the living presence of Paul D who embraces the tree on her back, her visible reminder of life and death—and hope: "'Aw, Lord, girl.' And he would tolerate no peace until he had touched every ridge and leaf of it with his mouth, none of which Sethe could feel because her back skin had been dead for years" (18). As they both embrace, he offers Sethe the chance to live in this/his world, the world of love and remembrance, the world of hope for some kind of tomorrow:

> Would there be a little space, she wondered, a little time, some way to hold off eventfulness, to push busyness into the corners of the room and just stand there a minute or two, naked from shoulder blade to waist, relieved of the weight of her breasts, smelling the stolen milk again and the pleasure of baking bread? Maybe this one time she could stop dead still in the middle of a cooking meal—not even leave the

stove—and feel the hurt her back ought to. Trust things and remember things because the last of the Sweet Home men was there to catch her if she sank? (18)

Can Sethe meld the pain of "stolen milk" with "the pleasure of baking bread"? Can the memory preserved free her present self from an increasingly isolated, denuded existence? Perhaps for Sethe, Paul D can assume her pain, his living presence can become the foundation for perseverance. He is attraction, an embraceable memory, a needed purpose in which to revive her muted spirit. And Paul D believes that he can move Sethe forward: "Merely kissing the wrought iron on her back had shook the house, had made it necessary for him to beat it to pieces. Now he would do more." He assumes an initiative for renewal and the confidence to overcome the horrors of memory; but there remains repulsion in the distance and separation of eighteen years: "His dreaming of her had been too long and too long ago. Her deprivation had been not having any dreams of her own at all" (20).

Their mutual desire in remembrance leads to silence and contradiction; "now they [are] sorry and too shy to make talk"; now there is difference and absence as neither character locates the unified self. "It [is] over before they [can] get their clothes off" (20). The passion imagined in Sethe's tree assumes a literal reversal for Paul D: ". . . the wrought-iron maze he had explored in the kitchen like a gold miner through pay dirt was in fact a revolting lump of scar" (21). Paul D yearns for a real tree, an "inviting tree"; he seeks another reality, a transcendence of present experience by submerging into the memory of Sweet Home:

> . . . trees were inviting; things you could trust and be near; talk to if you wanted to as he frequently did since way back when he took the midday meal in the fields of Sweet Home. (21)

For Paul D, word and image must solidify; when he remembers Sixto, another Sweet Home slave asleep beneath a tree, he thinks, "Now there was a man and that was a tree. Himself lying in the bed and the 'tree' lying next to him didn't compare" (22). He withdraws into this transcendental, essentialist past, seeking in it a prescribed, preconceived order. Yet he is a forward-looking man, hoping to build a future for himself and Sethe. His present is unsatisfactory; he remains intractable in the past, made inferior by his own essentialism. As much as Sethe, Paul D drifts within the paradox of a past and present self and place. The past is a necessary part of the present self; their stories need to be acknowledged so that living possibilities may be conceived. Yet an immersion into the past can also create stagnation and distortion, and may diminish or deny living possibilities.

Dreaming "too long" for word and image to materialize, Paul D's deprivation recedes into judgment and withdrawal. But even more contradictory is Sethe's recession into memory, for while her withdrawal is based upon not having any dreams "of her own at all," there is, in her memories of Sweet Home, a culmination in dream that reaches far beyond Paul D's relativist vision. Certainly there is, like Paul D, Sethe's sense of disillusion, but hers is located more precisely in the self and the place, and not, as with Paul D, in the disappointment of the Other. Sethe remembers that Sweet Home was never truly her home; she had had "six whole years of marriage to that 'somebody' son who had fathered every one of her children" (23). Unlike Baby Suggs, Sethe and Halle had been allowed for a time to keep each child so that they retained the appearances of a home. Yet neither this nor "a few yellow flowers on the table" (22) could make "a whitewoman's kitchen" (23) her own.

In retrospect, she believes "a bigger fool never lived" (24). But there remains a fluidity in her language of regret and grief. She had considered Sweet Home "a blessing she was reckless enough to take for granted"; she had never suffered the loss of a child like Baby Suggs; had never been treated to what her mother-in-law called ". . . the nastiness of life . . . upon learning that nobody stopped playing checkers just because the pieces included her children" (23). However, Sethe's own guilty sense of difference and illusion is displaced by imaginative dream that transcends fact and gives to memory an especial vitality. While gazing at Paul D's back, Sethe recalls a corn husking celebration at Sweet Home:

> As soon as one strip of husk was down, the rest obeyed and the ear
> yielded up to him its shy rows, exposed at last. How loose the silk.
> How quick the jailed-up flavor ran free.
>   No matter what all your teeth and wet fingers anticipated, there was
> no accounting for the way that simple joy could shake you.
>   How loose the silk. How fine and loose and free. (27)

Seemingly insignificant, Sethe's creative image expresses a desire that, in both form and content, pervades all of *Beloved*; it is the desire to break free from the sober, rational boundaries of material history. It is the desire that Virginia Woolf writes of in her "Women and Fiction": to "tear up all that we know human beings by, and fill those unrecognizable transparencies with such a gust of life that they transcend reality . . . [and] free life from its dependence on facts. . ." (132). In *Beloved*, the constant slippage into memory underscores and celebrates these "unrecognizable transparencies." These processes of consciousness demonstrate Sethe's and Morrison's desire to be "fine and loose and free" from the material, the realistic, and to concentrate on that which emits not a necessarily accurate reflection, but a "simple joy" to be retained, cherished and, most importantly, to be felt within the self, associational, embraceable, but shifting and variable, nebulous and dreamy.

According to Merle Rubin, "the opening of Toni Morrison's fifth novel is deliberately uninviting—an obstacle thrown in our path that puzzles and repels" (20). The language of memory and desire is the obstacle—now linear, now circular, now condensed, now displaced—that "puzzles and repels" us; we sense we know, but do not know, what we are reading; our expectations for simple resolutions of plot line are dislodged as Morrison produces the experience of personal history—chaotic, fragmentary, arbitrary, seemingly directionless. The novel's form, its plethoric obstructions, resist a coherent, unitary whole, and reflect Morrison's own desire to show, as she points out in an interview with Claudia Tate, that "every life to me has a rhythm, a shape—there are dips and curves as well as straightaways. You can't see the contours all at once" (124).

These narrative "obstacles" also have a duplicitous nature. While we may consider the revelations (and celebrations) of a history long denied as central to the novel, it becomes apparent that the ceaseless shifts of discourse within the text also play a salient role in its production.   In her interview with Tate, Morrison comments that in her novels

> . . . the language has to be quiet, it has to engage your participation. . . . It's not just telling the story; it's about involving the reader. . . . My language has to have holes and spaces so the reader can come into it. . . . He or she can feel something visceral, see something striking. Then we . . . come together to make this book, to feel this experience. It doesn't matter what happens. . . . I tell you at the beginning . . . what happen[s]. . . . (125)

By focusing attention on that which is felt within and around the contours of experience, Morrison sublates the story/history in her attempt to preserve it.   What is repressed, denied, ignored cannot be strictly told; it must be felt through the quiet engagement and chaos of language.   To embrace this story we must embrace its narrative dreaminess not as a means to stability and wholeness, but as a way of understanding that which cannot be embraced.

To embrace the dreams (and nightmares) within the past is to acknowledge and accept a more fully realized self and place. "Would it be all right?" Sethe thinks. "Would it be all right to go ahead and feel?" Can Sethe embrace the discursive subjectivity of her experience and thus project herself beyond her frozen time-space of 124 Bluestone Road—where ". . . all her effort [is] directed not on avoiding pain but on getting through it as quickly as possible" (38).   Paul D's living presence creates an embraceable desire in Sethe:

> He was responsible for that. Emotions sped to the surface in his company. Things became what they were: drabness looked drab; heat was hot. Windows suddenly had view. And wouldn't you know he'd be a singing man. (39)

This singing man expresses a confidence; he is able to freely articulate his experience; he commands a freedom of will and action; he is the "running man" who is conditioned by movement to anticipate possibilities, futures. To achieve possibility, he must impose an order, a sense of unity and meaning where none is perceived.   He must show mastery over the subject of his surroundings; he must create a stability that requires sustenation through his unfailing, singing confidence. In his position of knowledge and judgment, he takes action; he believes he can chase the ghost from the house, release Sethe from her disquietude, and imagine a future for them both. And thus, "with a table and a loud male voice he rid[s] 124 of its claim to local fame" (37).

With the ghost now exorcised, Paul D assumes complete responsibility for the lives of Sethe and Denver: "'Sethe, if I'm here with you, with Denver, you can go anywhere you want. Jump, if you want to, cause I'll catch you, girl. I'll catch you 'fore you fall'" (46). But the force of Paul D's presence—with his singing voice "too loud . . . for the little house chores he has engaged in" (40)—cannot allay the subversion of memory and death within the household; instead, his manly pride of dominance opens a channel to a different kind of flux and disquietude.

We are cued to this evasion of patriarchal design in the character of Denver. Already a lonely child, the absence/silence of a baby ghost leaves "Denver's world flat" (37). Years before she had seen her mother kneeling in prayer and kneeling beside her was "a white dress" which "had its sleeve around her mother's waist." Denver sees "two friendly grown-up women—one (the dress) helping out the other," and she recalls "the magic of her birth" (29), a story often told to her by Sethe. It is the story of Sethe's escape from Sweet Home after the sadistic "schoolteacher" had assumed control of the plantation. It is the story of a pregnant mother whose running has made her feet "so swollen she [can] not see her arch or feel her ankles" (29-30). It is the story of an exhausted, young woman who lies on the banks of the Ohio River and dreams about death in her womb, about never reuniting with her other children sent ahead to Baby Suggs. It is the story of Amy, a vagabond white girl looking for velvet, who massages Sethe's swollen feet and tells her, "'Anything dead coming back to life hurts'" (35). It is the story of the same white child who helps to deliver Denver on the banks of the Ohio; and in its entirety, it is a magical, miraculous testament to a mother's love and determination.

Sethe's story, told in increments to Denver throughout her childhood, plays a central role in continually energizing Denver's vision of her world; she is the inheritor of a story that is modulated by pain and death and dreams of life. And thus, as she returns her focus upon the scene, Sethe's "told story" (29) suggests to Denver that "maybe the white dress holding its arm around her mother's waist was in pain. If so, it could mean the baby ghost had plans" (35). Denver links her mother's pain and aspiration to the possibilities of life within the present, of the "plans" that Paul D has silenced and which have placed him in opposition to her appreciation for "the safety of ghost company." Neither he nor any of the past or present household, including Sethe, has tried to know or appreciate this safety which, for Denver, encompasses her "downright pleasure of enchantment" (37) in the memory and knowledge of the living past that resides in her mother's story. It is her source for imagination, a living, unfolding story that invigorates her spirit, that makes her feel "ripe and clear, and salvation [becomes] as easy as a wish" (29). This "'charmed child,'" as her mother calls her, identifies, in her inarticulated pulsations of "safety" and "pleasure," what we, as readers, will come to recognize and embrace as the novel's mythic/romantic superstructure.

It begins "as a little girl's houseplay"; Denver, as inheritor of her mother's story, creates her own vision within a self-imposed enclosure in the woods. In the bower of five boxwood bushes, Denver isolates herself from "the hurt of the hurt world" (29), and establishes her own kinship with memory and life. The bower contains a bottle of her mother's perfume, a gift given to her during the Civil War years, a gift that Denver steals because, for her, it provides a physical link to memory:

> One of the War years when Miss Bodwin, the white-woman, brought Christmas cologne for her mother and herself, oranges for the boys and another good wool shawl for Baby Suggs. Talking of a war full of dead people, she looked happy—flush-faced, and although her voice was heavy as a man's, she smelled like a roomful of flowers—excitement that Denver could have all for herself in the boxwood. (28)

Enclosed within her imaginative journey, Denver, in her own enchanted way, mirrors Sethe's lifelong journey—a journey, both physical and mental, that Sethe consciously wishes to sublimate, but which Denver persists in keeping alive through her confrontation with Paul D's mastery. With "sidelong looks" toward her mother, she asks Paul D "how long he [is] going to hang around." Paul D stands in the way of Denver's anticipated response to her continued call for the imaginative safety of memory and life. Sethe herself is "pleasantly troubled" (43) by Denver's recalcitrance. While she feels a mother's pride in her daughter's reenactment of a familiar defiance and determination, Sethe also knows that Denver's defiance stems from the interrupted flow of "plans" within the household. And while those "plans" appear to have an external source in the baby ghost, Sethe also stimulates their perpetuity with her own instructional and sublational discourse with Denver:

> "Some things go. Pass on. Some things just stay. I used to think it was my memory. You know. Some things you forget. Other things you never do. But it's not. Places, places are still there. . . .
> The picture is still there and what's more, if you go there—you who never was there—if you go there and stand in the place where it was, it will happen again; it will be there for you, waiting for you. So, Denver, you can't never go there. Never. Because even though it's all over—over and done with—it's going to always be there waiting for you." (35-6)

Sethe seeks to instruct Denver in the possibilities of a self and place; she creates anticipation for a connective past, and the "re" in her "rememory" denotes the Romantic fusion of a renewed, living memory where, as Denver comes to understand, "'nothing ever dies'" (37). Sethe's rememory now waits not only for her but also for her inheritor-daughter. Yet in the midst of anticipation, she negates her impulse to preserve rememory as she warns Denver never to approach what awaits her; that part of her continues to believe she must keep Denver "from the past that [is] still waiting. . ." (42).

To both preserve and deny, to both affirm and negate; these are the roles that Sethe feels compelled to assume; she is mindful of her story, in her rememory, and in transmitting it to Denver, she allows her to create an imaginative self that extends the possibilities for personal and cultural regeneration. But the paradox remains, what she has preserved and affirmed has also inflicted a dreadful emotional wound on her psyche, and thus, any transmission of her story, while it may enliven and nurture the self, may also distort and diminish living possibilities. If we, as readers, remain mystified by such a paradox, it is because, like Denver and Paul D, we cannot see the contours all at once. We must slowly come to feel the simple joy and monstrous knowledge enclosed in Sethe's rememory as a means of embracing the real and poetical reality of her personal history and perhaps more importantly, as a means to know more truly the self and place of a collective racial memory within a marginalized and oppressed history.

In a more transparent manner than in her previous novels, Morrison in *Beloved* infuses the "real" with the "magical," or what would be considered in the nineteenth century as a fusion of the "Novel" and the "Romance." In Nathaniel Hawthorne's "Preface" to his *The House of the Seven Gables*, he writes that the Novel

> . . . is presumed to aim at a very minute fidelity, not merely to the possible, but to the probable and ordinary course of man's experience. The [Romance] while, as a work of art, it must rigidly subject itself to laws, and while it sins unpardonably so far as it may swerve aside from the truth of the human heart—has fairly a right to present that truth under circumstances to a great extent, of the writer's own choosing or creation. (243)

Morrison accelerates her novel's continuing progress away from the "possible" and nearer to a distinct presentation of her "own choosing," while still "subjecting" the text "to laws" of "ordinary" reality. In the opening sentence of Chapter Five, the narrator introduces us to the baby ghost, now a young woman of nineteen years: "A fully dressed woman walked out of the water" (50). In introducing the baby ghost as a fully realized character, Morrison expresses her "right" in the substantial literary tradition of the "Romance" to create what Hawthorne calls in his "The Custom House," "a neutral territory, somewhere between the real world and fairyland, where the Actual and the Imaginary may meet, and each imbue itself with the nature of the other." This neutral territory encompasses the author's own multiple projections of experience liberated through the imagination where, as Hawthorne continues, the author may "dream strange things and make them look like the truth. . ." (45).

Beloved emerges from the water "sopping wet and breathing shallow"; and, as the narrator says, if anyone had seen her, "they would have hesitated before approaching her" (50), because in spite of her improbable, impossible appearance, she is smiling. She is this strange thing liberated as she emerges new born, fresh and flawless. As the inhabitants of 124 happen upon her in the woods, they marvel at her newness, her "new skin, lineless and smooth," her sleepy eyes which she struggles to keep open, her "baby hair" and her hands and feet, "soft and new" (50-52). At first, Beloved appears as a helpless, fully grown child, too weak from "fever" or "cholera" to express, or care for, herself. Initially unaware of her true identity, Sethe and Denver remain drawn to this "dreamy-eyed sleeping beauty" (53-4), and, out of kindness and compassion, they make every effort to shelter and comfort her.

In the weakness of Beloved's apparent illness there is an undercurrent of strength that is explicitly located by Paul D while carefully masked by a protective Denver. Paul D comments that she "'acts sick, sound sick, but she don't look sick,'" and he further claims that he "'[sees] her pick up the rocker with one hand.'" For her part, Denver protests that she didn't see "'no such thing'" (56). Their ongoing antipathy is moderated by Sethe who remains calm and mediative during the first days of Beloved's appearance. This contrast between household members becomes increasingly stark as both Paul D and Denver heighten their respective interrogative and protective behaviors.

Paul D seeks to unravel the mystery of Beloved's past: who were her relations, where did she come from, why is she wearing new shoes? At first Beloved responds vaguely, although innocently enough, to Paul D's questions; but in the midst of his continual questioning, Beloved erupts with a fury against his demand for certitude: "'I take the shoes! I take the dress! The shoe strings don't fix!' she shout[s] and give[s] him a look so malevolent Denver touch[es] her arm" (65). Beloved's presence in the household thwarts Paul D's unifying perceptions: "It had begun to look like a life. And damn! a water-drinking woman fell sick, got took in, healed, and hadn't moved a peg since" (66). Beloved continues to mystify Paul D; she is both presence and absence: "[He] had the feeling a large, silver fish had slipped from his hands the minute he grabbed hold of its tail" (65). But he also continues his interrogative pose; he expresses his dissatisfaction to Sethe and as they argue, Sethe maintains her medial position by emphasizing Beloved's apparently harmless presence and by stressing Paul D's new-found comfort and security. Yet he actually discounts this position in his need for certitude and subjective stability, and thus remains incapable of appreciating Beloved's elusive multiplicity.

Paul D's mystification is juxtaposed with Denver's own obsessional desire to harbor Beloved. She is especially drawn to Beloved, staying up with her while she sleeps; and whenever Sethe "intrudes" on them, Denver tells her, "'Leave us alone, Ma'am. I'm taking care of her.'" She is quickly overcome by a "breakneck possessiveness" (54) toward Beloved because Beloved seems to embody those "sweet secrets" of "a little girl's houseplay"; her presence affirms memory and life for Denver, and as such, she asks Beloved to never leave the farm and pointedly begs her not to tell Sethe of her identity. As the narrative proceeds, it becomes increasingly clear that Denver knows Beloved's identity, and later we learn that she shares "some monstrous and unmanageable dreams about Sethe" (103) that find release first in her fixation on the baby ghost and later in her desire to possessively retain a living bond with Beloved. Denver knows a deeper truth of death in her mother's memory; she knows, through neighborhood rumor and insinuation, that Sethe had murdered one of her children. And while this death has been left unspoken and thus repressed in Sethe's rememory, it is Denver who believes she keeps memory and life alive through her faith in the baby ghost and now in Beloved. For Denver, this means that "Beloved [is] *hers*" (104).

But Beloved demands that Sethe is the one she needs: "' You can go but she is the one I have to have.'" Out of desperation "against the threat of an unbearable loss" (76), Denver responds to Beloved's call for her mother's story. This is Denver's oppoortunity to perform the regenerative act, to pass on her mother's story and, in the process, to make the story truly her own to give. As she tells her mother's story, the story of her own birth, she begins to "see" and "feel" her story "through Beloved":

> Feeling how it must have felt to her mother. Seeing how it must have looked. And the more fine points she made, the more detail she provided, the more Beloved liked it. . . . The monologue became, in fact, a duet as they lay down together. (78)

The two create in their "duet" of call and response, a passionate, living sense of history that transcends any conventional history; as the narrator tells it, this oral interplay has the power of a lover "whose pleasure [is] to overfeed the loved." Felt and fluid, the scene is charged with communal rapture; "it [is] smelling like grass and feeling like hands — the unrested hands of busy women; dry, warm, prickly." Together, the two attempt to recreate their legacy, something, however, as the narrator continues, only Sethe can do because "she alone had a mind for it and the time afterward to shape it. . ." (78).

Throughout the early days of Beloved's presence on the farm, Sethe appears conspicuously detached from the appropriative strategies of Paul D and Denver. Quietly mediative, she exhibits no especial antipathy or endearment toward her. Yet subtly, Sethe, like Denver, "learn[s] the profound satisfaction Beloved [receives] from storytelling." Even though it "hurts" to tell Beloved of her past, Sethe finds herself "wanting to" and "liking it." Morrison uses oral imagery of nursing to underscore Beloved's hunger for a past, and "her thirst for hearing it" leaves Sethe pleased by Beloved's "open quiet devotion," pleased "the way a zealot pleases his teacher" (57).

Morrison deepens this visceral experience as Beloved's thirst for memory draws Sethe ever closer to her own rememory.

For the remainder of the novel, Beloved appears as a living receptacle for memory, a matrix for a past's distortive and creative possibilities, and through her mother she wishes to sustain herself as living memory. In one scene, Beloved pulls a tooth out of her mouth and thereby demonstrates her struggle to remain intact:

> Beloved looked at the tooth and thought, "This is it. Next would be her arm, her hand, a toe. Pieces of her would drop maybe one at a time, maybe all at once. . . . It is difficult keeping her head on her neck, her legs attached to her hips when she is by herself. (133)

Alone, Beloved remains an imaginary figure, formless and fluid, and Denver's inheritance is not enough to sustain her shape. That is why Beloved sorrowfully waits for Sethe to return from work and hungers for her mother's gaze and language to recreate her shape and stability. It is not, however, so simple as a mother's adored presence that may sustain Beloved. As memory, she formulates within the burdens of both love and hate, hope and fear, pain and pleasure. Thus Beloved is not (nor has she ever been) an entirely beneficent presence in the house. She hungers equally for the memories of both life and death; her prompting, prodding, propelling of Sethe's rememory requires a passive adoration/absorption as well as an actively malicious insistence for memory.

Beloved's loving insistence to be remembered, to regain a central form in Sethe's life is most clearly illustrated when Sethe sits down one day on Baby Sugg's "old preaching rock" (94). It is here that Baby had conducted Saturday services, where she taught a gospel of love and exhorted her neighborhood congregation to love their essential black selves: "'You've got to love it, *you*! . . . No, they don't love your mouth. You got to love it. This is flesh I'm talking about here. Flesh that needs to be loved. . ." (88). The reemergence of living memories at 124 have brought to Sethe "another kind of haunting" (96), and she longs to rekindle that exhortation to love; she longs to feel Baby's "fingers again on the back of [her] neck" and to "lay it all down" (95), all of the unspoken/unspeakable horrors of a collective racial memory. It is Baby Suggs whom

Sethe needs to turn to "for some kind of clarifying word; some advice about how to keep on with a brain greedy for news nobody could live with in a world happy to provide it" (95).

Early in the novel we learned that Baby Suggs had withdrawn from her doctrine of the body as the site of love and life. We later learn the reason for her withdrawal in the terrible knowledge of Sethe's violation of one of her own children's flesh. Throughout the novel, there are many remembrances of violation; the stories of its characters collectively encapsulate the cruel history of slavery: Baby Suggs is crippled for life, Halle is captured, humiliated, and presumed dead, Sixto is lynched and burned, Paul D is brutally imprisoned in a Georgia chain-gang. But enfolded within this collective tragedy is yet another kind of violation. It is the story of a frantic mother who will not allow her children to be returned to slavery and will not endure the same loss of her children that Baby Suggs was forced to endure. Sethe kills one of her four children before she is stopped, and here is "the news that nobody could live with"; here is "the haunting," the cruel paradox of memory as a restorative and distortive force, for how can Sethe find comfort in Baby's doctrine of love and life after violating it so grievously?

As Sethe continues to long for Baby Suggs, she begins to feel the "unmistakabl[e] caressing" (95) of Baby's presumed fingers. There is a soothing sense of recovery in her touch, a recovery of possibilities "when 124 was alive—she had women friends, men friends from all around to share grief with" (95-6). Suddenly, however, the fingers become stronger, more insistent, and "Sethe [is] actually more surprised than frightened to find that she [is] being strangled." When the fingers leave off, Sethe is perplexed that Baby would attempt to harm her, while Denver finds it impossible to believe: "'She wouldn't do that to you, Ma'am. Grandma Baby? Uh uh'" (96).

The unanticipated transformation from Sethe's comforting recovery to the unexplicable violation of self underscores the fluctuating quality and unresolvable paradox of memory. As Sethe knows, but does not wish to fully accept, memory is inseparably "a blessing" and "a haunting" (96), and Morrison further demonstrates its fluctuating quality by decentering the source of Sethe's pleasure and pain. She guesses it was Baby Suggs who tried to strangle her, but Denver wonders if perhaps it was Beloved. Following the incident, Beloved rubs her mother's aching neck and shoulders, and as the narrator says, Sethe's "walk-on-water life" (97), her superhuman effort to "beat back the past," gives way again to her increasing desire "to lay it all down." Following Denver's claim that she "saw" Beloved, she also returns to her state of captivated desire; she is "alarmed by the harm . . . Beloved plan[s] for Sethe, but [feels] helpless to thwart it, so unrestricted [is] her need to love another" (104).

The entire scene marks a progression from desire to trepidation to incertitude and back again to desire. In doing so, we see that Beloved has set in motion her own desired solidification of a remembered self. Even Paul D becomes a captive as Beloved seduces him and diffuses his influence on Sethe. He eventually leaves Sethe and 124 because he cannot reconcile his hope for order and continuity with his guilt and, more importantly, with his aversion toward Sethe when he learns of her monstrous secret. He is incapable of understanding maternal loss and how the potential for loss could compel a slave woman to become both a victim and an agent of a daemonic desire for familial survival.

But regardless of whether Beloved attracts or repels the household members, her destabilizing presence reinforces her growing centrality because it serves in gaining their recognition. She regains her name as she coerces Paul D into finally calling her "Beloved"; she stimulates their memories heretofore repressed or unknown to one another just as, in a larger sense, Morrison has created Beloved in order to acknowledge those nameless ones who died before they could pass on their stories.

Through destabilization and desire, Beloved regains her story, her spirit and voice, but in order for her to perpetuate them, she must envelop the only one who can truly nourish and preserve her presence. She yearns to exist and to be loved by her mother as a separate self; she needs to exist as an object of her mother's desire and love; yet she also yearns to exist as a subject fused with her mother into a single "hot thing," as she thinks: "I want to be there in the place where her face is and to be looking at it too" (210). When Sethe learns that Beloved is indeed her daughter, that she knows Sethe's song, she concludes that "whatever is going on outside my door ain't for me. The world is in this room. This here's all there is and all there needs to be" (183). Sethe is now fully resolved "to lay it all down"; she is contented to become engulfed only in the possibilities of memory. Overwhelmed with ideal mother-love, Sethe offers her own life to her daughter, as she tells herself, "I'll tend her as no mother ever tended a child, a daughter"; and she also expresses the desire to renew and re-create memory: "Now I can look at things again because she is here to see them too" (200-1).

Unlike Paul D, the living memory of Beloved offers Sethe a more appealing kind of renewal; rather than look forward into the possibilities of the present "real" world, she believes she can finally be "fine and loose and free" from the horrifying, isolating impingements of both a past and present world. She can preserve and sustain her memories as re-creations of a new ideal world. With Beloved, she too can experience the fusion of subject and object. "To be there" in the "world" of her "room," to "be looking at things again" will enable Sethe to truly embrace that which could not and cannot be embraced in either the past or present: "I can sleep like the drowned. . ." (204), Sethe believes, as she now immerses herself in the place of the many millions of slavery's victims and agents.

The memory of Beloved—a "drowned" collective memory—must be sustained and passed on by Sethe. Without her stories and others like them, her people can never hope to sustain themselves and their place with dignity and imagination. For Sethe what is rightfully hers, her Sweet Home, her journey to Baby Sugg's, her children, her Beloved, all of the memories repressed or silenced, need somehow to be released from their bonds of guilt and shame, need somehow to be given a purpose that ensures renewal and re-creation. In the insistence of mother-love and desire, Sethe and Beloved—their memories, their imaginations—merge until "it [is] difficult for Denver to tell who [is] who" (241). Memory does not expand beyond the contours of this self, but is left carefully preserved in subjective repetition. Sethe's desire for what is vital in memory, for that "simple joy" to be felt within the self demands attention, but yields no regenerative response: ". . . it was Beloved who made demands. Anything she wanted she got, and when Sethe ran out of things to give her, Beloved invented desire" (240).

Without reciprocation, Sethe becomes increasingly demoralized; her desire for memory in the isolated self permits only further guilt and self-loathing. The communally charged "duet" between Beloved and Denver is now reenacted in a distorted, destructive routine that has "Sethe plead[ing] for forgiveness, counting, listing again and again her reasons" (242). Sethe is willing to give up her life, to trade places with her Beloved, to unquestioningly satiate her hunger for stories and "sweets." But Beloved never gets "enough of anything" (240); she grows increasingly obese while continuing to "whine for sweets" (239), and her endless demands consume all of Sethe's emotional and physical strength until Denver sees "themselves beribboned, decked-out, limp and starving but locked in a love that [wears] everybody out" (243)l Sethe's love for that which cannot be embraced, her all-encompassing desire "to be there" alone in memory with Beloved and to thus renew what slavery has denied her, have served only to cancel all possibilities for life as a regenerative process. She remains frozen in a personal and historically collective tragedy that should but cannot affirm life: "This is not a story to pass on" (274), the narrator tells us at the close of the book; yet this same narrator has passed it on. How may one live with this paradox?

Perhaps the only response rests with the community, for as Sethe and Beloved demonstrate, a self and place cannot seem to survive and flourish without some form of reciprocal discourse. For nearly twenty years, Sethe's pride and shame intermixed with the community's fear and reproach have suspended any mutual social discourse. Ella, one of the more "practical" women in the community, sums up Sethe's and the community's contributions to this mutual estrangement: "She understood Sethe's rage in the shed . . . , but not her reaction to it, which Ella thought was prideful, misdirected. . . . When she got out of jail and made no gesture toward anybody . . . , Ella junked her and wouldn't give her the time of day." But it is also Ella who responds with the assertion that "rescue [is] in order" because "cogitation . . . cloud[s] things and prevent[s] action" (256). She resents what she calls this "invasion" that distorts possibilities because for her and the community, "the future [is] sunset; the past something to leave behind" (256).

What draws Ella to this pragmatic conclusion is Denver's reintegration into the community. In the midst of the on-going pastponement of 124, Denver decides to "step off the edge of [this] world" (243) and to call for help. Throughout her life she has sought some kind of life-sustaining shelter, in the bower and in the baby ghost; now, however, the shelter Denver seeks is from the women in the community. Beginning with her former teacher, Lady Jones, and expanding to include many other women, Denver reaches out for assistance and in the process becomes "inaugurated . . . in the world as a woman" (248). "All through the spring, names appear near or in gifts of food" (249) as the women offer their help and solace and demonstrate their "womanist" capacity for healing and integration. Gradually Denver is emboldened by their empathic response and she shares the story of her mother's plight. It takes several days for the women "to get the story properly blown up and themselves agitated and then to calm down and assess the situation" (255), but through their collective imaginations and practical assertions, they become inspired to respond to Denver's call with an understanding of and a compassion for the duplicitous intensity of Sethe's tortured past.

As thirty women stand before the house at Bluestone Road, their merging voices call to Sethe and her Beloved in sounds that reverberate with the same sorrow and pain of mother-love thwarted and disallowed:

> For Sethe it was as though the Clearing had come to her with all its heat and simmering leaves, where the voices of women searched for the right combination, the key, the code, the sound that broke the back of words. Building voice upon voice until they found it, and when they did it was a wave of sound wide enough to sound deep water and knock

the pods off chestnut trees. It broke over Sethe and she trembled like
the baptized in its wash. (261)

These singing women take "a step back to the beginning," to a
beginning that is just "sound" (259) which, through their
collective voicing, gains vitality and meaning. Before and
beyond words and reason, their merging voices reach into a
darkly fertile consciousness that consumes Sethe, as their
"sound" makes a spectral connection into that which cannot be
embraced. In a kind of reprise of the original tragedy,
Beloved is again dismissed by these singing women back to her
haunting past as Sethe and Denver run to the group and make
a hill: ". . . a hill of black people, falling" (262), falling
together in the human need for shared grief and consolation.

At the center of this communal expiation is Sethe's
misplaced revenge as she makes a desperate, pathetic attempt
to stab to death her kindly, white landlord, Mr. Bodwin. So
stricken is she with grief for being robbed of her child, she
lunges at an immediate symbol for schoolteacher, the plantation, and the whole of slavery's evil history. When Paul D and
his friend, Stamp Paid, discuss the incident, "its seriousness
and its embarrassment [make] them shake with laughter." It is
a laughter not made of derision, but of sorrow releasing itself
in search of dignity. For again, that is the basic desire
surrounding their stories; how do they attain dignity amidst
the terrible paradox of a past and present self and place?
When Paul D says to Stamp, "'Yeah, well, ain't we all [crazy]'"?
(265), he speaks of a craziness that emanates from the paradox.
The living memory both restores and destroys possibilities,
while its absence makes possibilities trivial and meaningless;
and neither immersion nor reciprocation can effectively close
this personal and collective wound.

As the novel closes, Sethe is left homeless; Mr. Bodwin has
decided to sell the haunted house. And she is once again
alone, muted, and waiting for death to come in Baby Suggs'
bed. When Paul D enters 124, "it is stone quiet," "a bleak and
minus nothing." As he sits down at the kitchen table, he
realizes that "something is missing from 124" (270); it is the
paradox that restores and distorts or, as Paul D thinks, it is "an

outside thing that embraces while it accuses" (271).   It is outside now because Sethe has taken to pondering colors like Baby Suggs; like Baby, she has relinquished her hold on the spirits of the past or the present as she tells Paul D, "'Oh, I don't have no plans. No plans at all'" (272). Paul D tries to comfort and reassure Sethe. "He wants to put his story next to hers," to be joined with her in a struggle for survival and for, as he says, "'some kind of tomorrow'" (273). He tells Sethe that she and not Beloved is her own "best thing," but in her response, "'Me? Me?'" (273), there lingers too much hope and too much despair.

Conclusion

The complex range of emotions within which Morrison writes constitutes a tenuous balance between negation and affirmation of selfhood and place within the community. Her characters waver within the contradictions and ambiguities of desire and repression, control and chaos, attraction and repulsion, connection and withdrawal. Within this atmosphere of irresolution, there lingers a measure of despair that seems to negate all hope for renewal. Pecola is victimized into insanity; Sula is ostracized into inertia and death; Pilate must recreate a world apart; Jadine is repulsed by a mythic past; and Sethe is marooned in doubt. In short, each character is unable to find and make a fully realized self and place because each has been in some way warped by communal circumstances.

Yet for each circumstance comes a measure of affirmation that points to the potential for cultural regeneration. Through memory and story, dream and song, each of Morrison's narratives continually focuses beyond the isolated, dystopian self and toward the potentialities of a desired, collective self. This collective self finds expression in Claudia's neighborhood retrospection, in Nel's cognitional cry, and in Pilate's stories and songs; it attains a hopeful realization in Milkman's search to embracement, in Son's utopian retreat, in Paul D's consolation, and most certainly in Sethe's rememory of communal joys and sorrows.

These characters acknowledge, however vaguely, that they must search for identity by returning to the neighborhood and to the communal experience. They do so in order, as Morrison has said, "to survive whole in a world where [they] are all . . . victims of something" (Bakerman 60). Thus, the community, for better or worse, has the power to become the site of renewal for its members. Their response to the call of communal experience determines forever their course in life, and allows them a significant measure of hope and comfort and wholeness in an otherwise alienating and lonely world of victims and victimizers.

There can indeed be, then, "a joy and protection in the clan"; a joy and protection that exists not only as a release from the vicissitudes of daily living, but more importantly, a joy and protection that functions as a sustainer and a shaper of identity. In depicting a totality of communal emotions and experience, Morrison's novels demonstrate that the community is a multiple, refractory space within each self which, as it dispossesses and nurtures, deceives and instructs, assails and comforts, serves as the ultimate touchstone in the search for self and place.

List of Works Cited

Primary Sources

Morrison, Toni. *Beloved*. New York: Knopf, 1987.

___. *The Bluest Eye*. New York: Pocket, 1970.

___. "City Limits, Village Values: Concepts of the Neighbor-hood in Black Fiction." *Literature and the Urban Experience.* Ed. Michael C. Jaye and Ann Chalmers Watts. New Brunswick: Rutgers UP, 1981a. 35-43.

___. *Song of Solomon*. New York: Signet, 1977.

___. *Sula*. New York: Plume, 1973.

___. *Tar Baby*. New York: Signet, 1981b.

Interviews

Bakerman, Jane. "The Seams Can't Show: An Interview with Toni Morrison." *Black American Literature Forum.* 7 (Summer 1978): 60.

Stepto, Robert B. "Intimate Things in Place: A Conversation with Toni Morrison." *Massachusetts Review.* (Sept. 1977): 473-89.

Tate, Claudia. "Conversation with Toni Morrison." *Black Women Writers at Work*. New York: Continuum, 1983. 117-131.

Secondary Sources

Feminist/Women's Studies:

Beale, Frances. "Double Jeopardy: To Be Black and Female." *The Black Women*. Ed. Toni Cade. New York: New American Library, 1970. 90-100.

Bethel, Lorraine. "This Infinity of Conscious Pain: Zora Neale Hurston and the Black Female Literary Tradition." *But Some of Us Are Brave*. Eds. Gloria T. Hull, Patricia Bell Scott, and Barbara Smith. Old Westbury, NY: The Feminist P, 1982. 176-188.

Christian, Barbara. "A Promise Song." *Black Women Novelists: The Development of a Tradition, 1892-1976*. Westport, CT: Greenwood P, 1980a. 137-179.

___. *Black Feminist Criticism: Perspectives on Black Women Writers*. New York: Pergamon, 1985a.

de Beauvoir, Simone. *The Second Sex*. New York: Vintage P, 1974.

Higginbotham, Elizabeth. "The Representative Issues in Contemporary Sociological Work on Black Women." *But Some of Us Are Brave: Black Women Studies*. Eds. Gloria T. Hull, Patricia Bell Scott, and Barbara Smith. Old Westbury, NY: The Feminist P, 1982. 93-98.

hooks, bell. *Ain't I A Woman: Black Women and Feminism*. Boston: South End P, 1981.

Hurston, Zora Neale. "How It Feels to be Colored Me." *I Love Myself When I Am Laughing. And Then Again When I Am Looking Mean and Impressive: A Zora Neale Hurston Reader*. Ed. Alice Walker. New York: The Feminist P, 1979. 152-55.

___. *Their Eyes Were Watching God*. Urbana: U of Illinois P, 1978.

___. *The Sanctified Church*. Berkeley: Turtle Island, 1983.

Ladner, Joyce. *Tomorrow's Tomorrow*. Garden City, NY: Anchor, 1972.

Lerner, Gerda. *Black Women in White America: A Documentary History*. New York: Vintage P, 1972.

Ogunyemi, Chikwenye Okonjo. "Womanism: The Dynamics of the Contemporary Black Female Novel in English." *Signs* 11 (Autumn 1985): 63-80.

Smith, Barbara. "Toward a Black Feminist Criticism." *But Some of Us Are Brave: Black Women's Studies*. Ed. Gloria T. Hull, Patricia Bell Scott, and Barbara Smith. Old Westbury, NY: The Feminist P, 1982. 157-75.

Walker, Alice. *In Search of Our Mothers' Gardens*. San Diego: Harcourt, Brace, Jovanovich, 1983.

Walker, Alice. "On Refusing to be Humbled by Second Place in a Contest You Did Not Design: A Tradition by Now." *I Love Myself When I Am Laughing, And Then Again When I Am Looking Mean and Impressive: A Zora Neale Hurston Reader*. New York: The Feminist P, 1979. 1-5.

Washington, Mary Helen. "Teaching Black-Eyed Susans: An Approach to the Study of Black Women Writers." *But Some of Us Are Brave: Black Women's Studies*. Ed. Gloria T. Hull, Patricia Bell Scott, and Barbara Smith. Old Westbury, NY: The Feminist P, 1982. 208-217.

___. "Zora Neale Hurston: A Woman Half in Shadow." *I Love Myself When I Am Laughing, And Then Again When I Am Looking Mean and Impressive: A Zora Neale Hurston Reader*. Ed. Alice Walker. New York: The Feminist P, 1979. 7-25.

Woolfe, Virginia. "Jane Eyre and Wuthering Heights." *Women and Writing*. London: The Women's P, 1979. 126-32.

General

Baker, Houston A. *Long Black Song: Essays in Black American Literature and Culture*. Charlottesville: UP of Virginia, 1972.

Baldwin, James. *No Name in the Street*. New York: Dell, 1973.

___. *Notes of a Native Son*. Boston: Bacon, 1962.

Cleaver, Eldridge. "Notes on a Native Son." *Soul on Ice*. New York: Dell, 1968. 97-111.

Du Bois, W.E.B. "Negro Art." *Crisis* 22 (June 1921): 55-6.

Ellison, Ralph. "The Art of Fiction: An Interview." *Shadow and Act*. New York: Signet, 1966a. 169-183.

___. *Invisible Man*. New York: Random House, 1952.

___. "Richard Wright's Blues." *Shadow and Act*. New York: Signet, 1966b, 89-104.

Gates, Henry Louis, Jr. "Preface to Blackness: Text and Pretext." *Teaching Afro-American Literature: The Reconstruction of Instruction*. Eds. Dexter Fisher and Robert B. Stepto. New York: MLA, 1969. 44-69.

Gayle, Addison, Jr. *The Way of the New World: The Black Novel of America*. Garden City, NY: Anchor P, 1975.

Howells, William Dean. "Review of *Majors and Minors*." *W. D. Howells as Critic*. Ed. Edwin H. Cady. London: Routledge and Kegan Paul, 1973. 251.

Hughes, Langston. "The Negro Artist and the Racial Mountain." *Black Expression: Essays by and About Black Americans in the Creative Arts.* Ed. Addison Gayle, Jr. New York: Weybright and Talley, 1969. 258-263.

Jefferson, Thomas. *Notes on the State of Virginia.* London: Stockdale, 1787.

Joans, Ted. "Ted Joans: Tri-Continental Poet." *Transition* 48 (1975): 4-12.

Johnson, James Weldon, ed. *Book of American Negro Poetry.* New York: Harcourt, Brace, 1931.

Jordan, Jane. "On Richard Wright and Zora Neale Hurston." *Black World* 23 (Aug 1974): 4-8.

Karenga, Ron. "Black Cultural Nationalism." *The Black Aesthetic.* Ed. Addison Gayle, Jr. Garden City, NY: Doubleday, 1971. 32-38.

Klotman, Phyllis Rauch. *Another Man Gone: The Black Runner in Contemporary Afro-American Literature.* Port Washington, NY: Kennikat P, 1977.

O'Meally, Robert G. "Riffs and Rituals: Folklore in the Work of Ralph Ellison." *Teaching Afro-American Literature: The Reconstruction of Instruction.* Eds. Dexter Fisher and Robert B. Stepto. New York: MLA, 1979. 153-169.

Reed, Ishmael. *Yellow Back Radio Broke Down.* Garden City, NY: Doubleday, 1969.

Reilly, John M. "History-Making Literature." *Studies in Black American Literature: Belief vs. Theory in Black American Literary Criticism.* Greenwood, FL: Penkevill P, 1984. 85-119.

___. "The Reconstruction of Genre as Entry into Conscious History." *Black American Literature Forum* 13 (1979): 3-6.

Shange, Ntozake. "taking a solo/a poetic responsibility/a poetic imperative." *Nappy Edges*. New York: St. Martin's P, 1978. 2-12.

Smith, William Gardner. "The Negro Writer: Pitfalls and Compensations." *The Black Novelist*. Ed. Robert Hemenway. Columbus, OH: Charles E. Merrill, 1970. 198-204.

Stepto, Robert B. "Temenos/Notes on a Course." *Teaching Afro-American Literature: The Reconstruction of Instruction*. Eds. Dexter Fisher and Robert B. Stepto. New York: MLA, 1979. 17-23.

Wright, Richard. "Between Laughter and Tears: A Review of *Their Eyes Were Watching God*." *New Masses* (5 Oct 1937): 22, 25.

___. "Blueprint for Negro Writing." *The Black Aesthetic*. Ed. Addison Gayle, Jr. Garden City, NY: Doubleday, 1971. 333-45.

___. "The Literature of the Negro of the United States." *Black Expression*. Ed. Addison Gayle, Jr. New York: Weybright and Talley, 1969. 198-229.

Morrison

The Bluest Eye

Miner, Madonne M. "Lady No Longer Sings the Blues: Rape, Madness, and Silence in *The Bluest Eye*." *Conjuring: Black Women, Fiction, and Literary Tradition*. Eds. Marjorie Pryse and Hortense J. Spillers. Bloomington: Indiana UP, 1985. 176-91.

Sula

Banyiwa-Horne, Naana. "The Scary Face of the Self: An Analysis of the Character of Sula in Toni Morrison's *Sula*." *Sage* 2 (Spr. 1985): 28-31.

Tar Baby

Caplan, Brina. "Review of *Tar Baby*." *The Nation* (2 May 1981): 529-530.

Mobley, Marilyn E. "Narrative Dilemma: Jadine as Cultural Orphan in Toni Morrison's *Tar Baby*." *The Southern Review* 23 (Autumn 1989): 761-70.

Sheed, Wilfrid. "Review of *Tar Baby*." *Atlantic Monthly* (Apr 1981): 119.

Beloved

Rubin, Merle. "Review of *Beloved*." *The Christian Science Monitor* (5 Oct 1987): 20.

Selected Novels

Turner, Darwin T. "Theme, Characterization, and Style in the Works of Toni Morrison." *Black Women Writers (1950-1980): A Critical Evaluation*. Ed. Mari Evans. Garden City, NY: Anchor-Doubleday, 1984. 361-69.

Willis, Susan. "Eruptions of Funk: Historizing Toni Morrison." *Black American Literature Forum* 16 (Spr 1982): 34-42.

Additional Sources

Barthes, Roland. *Mythologies*. New York: Hill and Wang, 1972.

Hawthorne, Nathaniel. "The Custom House." *The Scarlet Letter*. New York: Signet, 1959. 15-53.

___. "Preface" to *The House of the Seven Gables*. New York: Random House, 1965. 243-44.

Jameson, Frederic. *Marxism and Form: Twentieth Century Dialectical Theories of Literature*. Princeton UP, 1971.

Roudiez, Leon S. "Introduction." Julia Kristeva's *Desire In Language: A Semiotic Approach to Literature and Art.* Ed. Leon S. Roudiez. New York: Columbia UP, 1980. 1-20.

Sartre, Jean-Paul. *Being and Nothingness.* New York: Citadel P, 1966.